W9-CHF-544

STREETS

OF GEORGE TOWN

PENANG

Designed & Produced by Janus Print & Resources
Colour separated and printed in Penang, Malaysia

To order, contact
Janus Print & Resources
120 Armenian Street,
10200 Penang, Malaysia
tel 04-2633985 • fax 04-2633970
email lubisksn@pd.jaring.my • lubisksn@tm.net.my

Discounts are available for bulk orders,
schools and non-profit organisations.

Perpustakaan Negara Malaysia Cataloguing-in-Publication Data

Khoo, Su Nin
Streets of George Town Penang / text & photographs by Khoo Su Nin.

Bibliography: p.
ISBN 983-9886-00-2
1. Streets--Pulau Pinang--Georgetown--Guidebooks
2. Georgetown (Pulau Pinang)--Description--Views.
3. Georgetown (Pulau Pinang)--History.
I. Title.
915.95113

PREFACE TO THE THIRD EDITION

George Town has been described as 'a living heritage city' and a place of historical 'cultural fusion', with great potential for educating a whole new generation about Asian civilizations, architectures and historical cultural transformation.

In 1999, George Town, Penang, was listed by the World Monuments Watch as one of the World's Hundred Most Endangered Sites. The World Monuments Fund, a prominent New York-based philantrophic organisation, is calling the world's attention to the precious and precarious state of the Penang's heritage.

At the same time, the Malaysian federal authorities have announced their intention to nominate Penang and Malacca jointly to the UNESCO World Heritage list. The UNESCO World Heritage Convention signed by member nations is an international convention to conserve the most outstanding natural and/or cultural heritage sites in the world for all humanity and posterity.

In the last few years, we have witnessed growing recognition among international conservationists that George Town, Penang, represents what is probably the most sizeable and culturally diverse built heritage ensemble left in Southeast Asia. Yet locally, our commitment to this heritage wavers.

Penang was ill-prepared for the Repeal of the Rent Control Act at the turn of the millennium, which has accelerated the decline and decantation of the old city centre. Formed in January 2000, a group called Save Our Selves (SOS) is mobilizing former rent control tenants to respond to the crisis. The Penang Heritage Trust (PHT) and the Consumers' Association of Penang (CAP) have also provided advisory services to government, tenants and landlords alike.

The government has responded to the heritage and housing crisis, better late than never. Housing is being offered to the hardcore urban poor. It is hoped that the RM100 million fund (RM80 million federal loan and RM20 million state grant) for the rehabilitation of formerly rent controlled houses for social housing will also achieve results as a conservation incentive. Notwithstanding, the overall response of the Penang government and society to historical threat and opportunity is still grossly inadequate. Many alarming trends continue unchecked.

With the Repeal of Rent Control, the city is quickly losing its heritage character through ubiquitous renovations and defacement as well as outright demolitions. Buildings are deteriorating rapidly after their inhabitants move out. Vacant properties are being speculated upon, illegal warehousing is rampant.

Communities are being broken up, traditional trades are disappearing. With tenants moving out *en masse*, family heirlooms and documents are being lost or dispersed. George Town, the largest repository of urban heritage in the country, is being liquidated as antiques and real estate.

All over Penang and Malaysia, prewar

buildings are still being demolished without due consideration of their history, heritage, educational and tourism values. Only few examples that appear in this book will be alluded to.

Within the oldest part of George Town, the grid planned by Francis Light, the corner of Bishop Street and King Street (p.102) has been flattened. The ancient-looking undertakers' row on Carnarvon Street (p.62) has made way for a car park. An international alert on CNN did not succeed in stopping the demolition of six houses on Beach Street, attached to the Boon San Tong Khoo Kongsi at Victoria Street (p.164).

When it was rumoured that Morningside, former residence of Cheah Kee Ee on Burmah Road (p.54), had been identified for conservation, it was promptly demolished for a carpark. Pangkor Road has lost its Dutch Art Deco cottages (p.138). Seven government quarters buildings at Leith Street Ghaut were illegally demolished for a hotel development. The few remaining buildings along Farquhar Street which originally housed the St. George's Girls' School in 1888 were razed by fire (p.87, 107).

Although the rate of demolition has slowed down compared with the boom period of pre-1997, it is expected to speed up with the eviction of tenants after the Repeal of Rent Control. The historic city of George Town is more vulnerable than ever to marring new erections and destructive building practices.

Insensitive earthworks on adjacent properties have caused great anguish to the worshippers at the Benggali Mosque and the owners of the Cheong Fatt Tze Mansion on Leith Street (p.104). Earthworks and clearing works in the vicinity of Leith Street Ghaut

(p.108) has been linked to the collapse of the early 19th century brick aquaduct (p.86). The destabilisation and cracking of more than 300 prewar houses in its vicinity—of which dewatering caused by the construction of the Prangin Mall (p.151) has been alleged as the most probable cause—is a case study in urban disaster.

While heritage awareness has swept Penang in the last few years, technical education about the care of old buildings has hardly reached the vernacular-speaking members of the building industry. As a direct result, careless renovations have destroyed countless heritage buildings. The once handsome Anglo-Indian Godown at Penang Street (p.143) lost much of its original character when its wooden shutters were replaced with asbestos panels. The Ch'ng Teong Swee Mansion at Anson Road (p.29) with its beautiful stucco detailing has been absolutely defaced.

Cosby Hall on Macalister Road (p.122) was renovated for use as a college building, but not with as much sympathy as was done with the neighbouring Armenian house originally belonging to the Anthonys. The Yap Kongsi (p.32) has refurbished its premises and organised an exhibition of its history. When the Yap Kongsi added ornate new dragon pillars, the Kheng Chew Association (Hainanese Temple) was inspired to do the same (p.128), without bothering about the distinctions between Hokkien and Hainanese architectural styles.

The authorities have made no apparent attempt to discourage the rapid erosion of heritage caused by the scraping away of stucco decorations, the changing of terracotta roofs to zinc or asbestos, the removal of antique doors, the replacement of timber window shutters with glass and aluminium, the gutting out of interiors, or the use of incompatible and potentially destructive materials. Water-sealing cement normally used for swimming pools has been applied over the porous brick surfaces of such important monuments as the St. George's Church (p.87), the Cathedral of the Assumption (p.90) and even the City Hall (p.85). Only time can tell the results.

Local technical know-how is certainly not lacking. The Syed Alatas Mansion received a prestigious conservation award from Badan Warisan Malaysia. The Cheong Fatt Tze Mansion (p. 106) has been lovingly conserved in a Grade 1 Restoration, which won the UNESCO Asia Pacific Heritage Awards 2000, and is now an exclusive hotel.

The restoration of the Acheen Street Mosque (p.25) and the Khoo Kongsi Theatre, both funded by the Federal Government, also won conservation awards. Government buildings like the Penang State Museum (p.89) and the old Central Fire Station has been spruced up by the Public Works Department. This year, the National Museum is investing in the restoration of Fort Cornwallis on Light Street (p.109) and the Captain Kling Mosque on Pitt Street (p.148).

The restoration and renewal of Convent Light Street (p.112), spearheaded by the Convent's old girls, has been Penang's largest community-driven conservation project ever. The magnificent Khoo Kongsi temple is being restored (p.61), even as the uneasy atmosphere of tenant protest fills Cannon Square.

New uses have been found for old buildings. The five houses on Leith Street opposite the Cheong Fatt Tze Mansion as well as a row of eight houses on Krian Road have been converted into pubs and restaurants. For many years a fire site, a former hotel at 100 Cintra Street has been rehabilitated into a crafts bazaar. The former Wearne Brothers' car showroom, a large columnless space, has been adapted into a heritage-themed shopping mall called *The Garage*. The former government quarters on Burmah Road (p. 54) have been restored and gentrified, while similar rows along Immigration Road and Chow Thye Road have been turned into boutique hotel, shops and offices. The Foo Tye Sin Mansion on Light Street (p.110) has been restored as a bank, while the ABN Bank on Beach Street (p.46) has been converted into an elegant café. Boustead has renovated its offices on Weld Quay (p.170), while another shipping office was smartly renovated by the British Council into a language centre.

The Penang Heritage Trust itself has carried out small-scale restorations such as the Protestant Cemetery at Northam Road (p.131), a splendid re-roofing of the Carpenters' Guild or Loo Pun Hong on Love Lane (p.120), the repainting of the Shaikh Zachariah Basheer house, a family waqf, at 67 Acheen Street. Suffolk House in Ayer Itam has finally secured the transfer of land and a government starting grant for urgent works (p.40).

The Trust also produced a souvenir album to show how the Hollywood Movie 'Anna and the King' made use of Penang's heritage locations – the Syed Alatas Mansion and the small corner park at Armenian Street (p.30), Soo Hong Lane (p.157), Swettenham Pier, the Khoo Kongsi (p.61) and the Town Hall (p.84).

Eight years after it was first announced, the local government finally insists that they are going to do something about the revitalization of Armenian Street and Acheen Street. One end of Acheen Street has been repainted in bright colours through public sector initiative and private sector cooperation. The city has implemented its first semi-pedestrian mall project known as the "Campbell Street Mall", about ten years after it was drawn up with the assistance of urban designers from the Yokohama City Council, but public response has been less than enthusiastic.

To spur revitalization, the local government would hopefully put its heritage buildings into better use. The King Edward Memorial Hospital on Macalister Road and its extensive grounds, meant to be used for the public good, is now a blighted landscape. About 30 art and community groups are jointly urging the local government to return the Penang Town Hall to the original civic and cultural use (p.84). One year after the first call in August 1999, the Town Hall is still not available for booking as a venue for public events.

Due to poor security, the Protestant Cemetery has been repeatedly vandalised. The proposed relocation of the Prangin Road (p.152), Chowrasta and Campbell Street (p.58) markets will adversely affect local women and elderly pedestrians, as well as the surrounding small traders whose livelihoods are tied to the market.

The courthouse and Logan's Memorial on Light Street (p.116) may soon be obscured by a proposed courthouse extension. Several yuppie lawyers have stated their preference for the convenience of an adjacent carpark over the memory of a historical figure who has contributed immeasurably to Penang society.

For heritage to survive beyond the market-driven present, a path needs to be carefully steered between obsolescence and dereliction on the one hand, and tourism and gentrification on the other. In the meantime, a lot of new kitch heritage is replacing the real thing. The Town House at No. 1 Penang Road is a victim of facadism or facadomy.

Most of the original E&O Hotel (p.90) has been demolished, retaining only the facade, dome and eastern wing. Even the 1903 ballroom, where many of Penang's balls, social events and marriages took place, was sacrificed. After a few years of dereliction, the hotel has now been glamorously reinvented and its services upgraded to cater to 21st century cultural tourism.

Northam Road (p.129-137), formerly Millionaire's Row, paints the decline of Penang's old families and the loss of a gracious era. It also presents a picture of ad hoc planning, misguided guidelines, and futile attempts to balance development with conservation under such circumstances. Fully air-conditioned highrise blocks have replaced yesterday's airy and fanciful mansions. A corporate concrete jungle is taking advantage of, and encroaching upon, Northam Road's lush green environs.

A heart-wrecking sight is Hardwicke, badly brutalised and then hastily mended, now a humble gatehouse or footstool to a towering new highrise. Only Homestead and Woodville have been maintained by the old families, while Leong Yin Kean Mansion is being restored by Escoy Smelting. The future of the wonderfully unique Anglo-Chinese Shih Chung School, the Yeoh Cheang Seng Villa, Soonstead, The Aloes, Runnymede and many other grand buildings are uncertain.

After its illegal demolition on Christmas day in 1993, the great significance of Asdang House aka Metropole Hotel for Penang's links with Thai royal history is just being appreciated.

Gurney Drive, a popular promenade, may be reclaimed by 0.8 km, If so, the highrise condos blocking the sea view and breeze may suffer the same fate they imposed on others. With the recent influx of Indonesian Chinese residents, Pulau Tikus has turned into a posh suburb — the 'Bangsar' of Penang. The former Jewish residence dated 1918, at the corner of Cantonment and Kelawai Road, has been proudly restored by a private owner. Although Kampong Serani is tragically gone, with some foresight middle-class Penang can yet redeem what is left of Pulau Tikus's country villas and its rich heritage of Eurasian, Arab, Thai, Burmese and Straits Chinese minorities.

Several jewels of Penang's history have yet to be saved. The Chung Keng Kwee Temple, Hai Kee Chan Townhouse (p. 76) and the Chung Thye Pin Villa in Relau are derelict and at risk. The Art Deco Rex Cinema on Burma Road and the Majestic Cinema nearby are up for sale.

Birch House and Chin Ho Square are deserted after the closure and relocation of the ESCOY plant, formerly known as Eastern Smelting, which has been operating at Datuk Keramat Road (p.83) since 1908. This spells the end of a chapter for what was probably the most significant institution in Penang's 20th century industrial history.

Penang Hill has been temporarily saved, but now there is again talk of highland development and cable car. Many heritage trees have been chopped down for road-widening, and practically no new parks gazetted in the city. With rapid development, erosion of hill slopes and river sedimentation, the flood-prone areas in George Town are ever increasing and flash floods are worsening. The river that bears the name of Penang – the Pinang River that flows through George Town — has been awarded the distinction of being Malaysia's dirtiest river.

The crisis of heritage and environment also represents the spiritual crisis ushered in by globalised greed. Everywhere, trustees of religious properties and guild properties are talking about going into joint ventures for development at the expense of existing local community.

The battles for the College-General and Kampong Serani -- the Eurasian heartlands -- have been fought and lost, while the Catholic Church still has vast tracts of settled land to sell.

Every now and then there are proposals to redevelop waqf land, which also happen to be the main repositories of Muslim heritage in Penang. Most proposals are ignorant or knowingly disrespectful of the Islamic syariah law and the wills of the benefactor. In response to one such proposal, the qariah council of the Simpang Enam Mosque at Macalister Road (p.121) staged a protest against the redevelopment of its 100 year old mosque endowment and took the case to court. Meanwhile, the historic tombs of two generous Muslim benefactors, Capitan Kling Cauder Mydin Merican at Kampong Kolam (p.97) and Mohamed Merican Noordin at Chulia Street (p.73) are still in ruins. The burnt-out Darul Ehsan Football Club at Kampong Kolam is a hide-out for drug addicts and vermin.

For the sake of profit, the descendants of Khoo Soo Hong (p.157) have allowed developers to exhume the family burial ground at Bagan Jermal/Mount Erskine and construct four blocks of highrise flats. After a court battle, the developers agreed to relocate the ornately decorated tomb of Khoo Soo Hong (died 1895), bearing carved stone panels depicting Confucius's 24 filial pieties, to one corner of the lot. So much for Confucian values.

The original tiered gardens of Kek Lok Si Temple (p.37) which attracted far-away pilgrims and travellers since the day it was built, has been concretized and awfulized by overbuilding. If spiritualism can be so easily traded for crass commercialism under the watchful eyes of enlightened buddhas, than human beings are pretty much in the same predicament as the tortoises in the Kek Lok Si's 'Liberation Pond'.

As George Town is endangered, so is our human diversity. The efforts to recover our heritage and cultural memory, tangible and intangible, are only just beginning.

Useful Contacts

Penang Heritage Trust (PHT)
26-A Stewart Lane
10200 Penang
Tel 604-2642631, 604-2645487
Fax 604-2642631
Email phtrust@po.jaring.my
Website www.pht.org.my
PHT offers guided heritage tours, advice on heritage buildings and information about conservation in Penang.

Asia & West Pacific Network for Urban Conservation (AWPNUC)
c/o Penang Heritage Trust (The Secretariat)
Website www.awpnuc.org

Badan Warisan Sumatra
Abdur-Razzaq Lubis
Malaysian Representative
120 Armenian Street
10200 Penang
Tel 604-2620123
Fax 604-2633970
Email arlubis@mandailing.org
Website www.mandailing.org
            www.sumatra-heritage.org.id

Dr. Sun Yat Sen's Penang Base
120 Armenian Street
10200 Penang
Tel 604-2620123
Fax 604-2633970
Email lubisksn@tm.net.my
Exhibition on Dr. Sun Yat Sen in Penang (English and Mandarin) in a traditional Straits Chinese house, venue of the Penang Conference (1910) where the Canton Uprising (1911) was planned.

PREFACE *TO THE* SECOND EDITION

Since the book was released last year, many heritage buildings have fallen and many concrete towers have risen in George Town.

Metropole Hotel alias Asdang House (p. 135) was illegally demolished over Christmas. The Leong Yin Kean Mansion (p. 136) will soon be auctioned while the Shih Chung School (p. 133) property has changed hands and the school is being relocated. The Yeoh Cheang Seng Villa (p. 130), Hardwicke, Soonstead and The Aloes (p. 134-135) face an uncertain future. With several new highrises, including one which has been described as resembling an "orthopaedic boot", Northam Road or Jalan Sultan Ahmad Shah is doomed to road widening, entailing the loss of heritage trees.

The Eurasian village or Kampung Serani at Pulau Tikus (p. 57) has been levelled for condominiums. The house along Macalister Road (p. 14) has burnt down. The mansion of Ch'ng Teong Swee (the author's maternal grandfather) at Anson Road (p. 29) was sold by the family and its fate is unknown.

The United Muslim Association (p. 162) will soon be redeveloped. Several rows of shophouses (p. 19) have been demolished and the Prangin Market (p. 152) will be relocated to make way for yet more KOMTAR-spawned development.

Insiders say that changes to the Rent Control Act will be tabled in Parliament shortly after the upcoming elections. Booming property prices resulting from speculation and foreign investment make the conservation cause increasingly difficult.

A seven-storey building has defied Municipal Council guidelines by raising its mock-Italian head in Chulia Street to blot out the vista of the Wisma Kastam clocktower (p. 67). While the importance of Chulia Street as a tourist milieu remains gravely underrated, the neighbourhood faces mounting development pressure.

In line with government taste, the Court Buildings on Light Street (p. 116) and the City Hall at the Esplanade (p. 85), like the Governor's Residency (p. 155), have been decked with bright blue corrugated roofs. The Malaysian fashion for blue tops was first set by royal palaces of various states.

The STAR office (p. 153) maintains an aluminum mask over its Pitt Street facade. The Tengku Kudin House (p. 163) will be converted into a mess hall for the marine police. There are new concrete structures in the Penang Botanic Gardens.

The western wing of the Convent Light Street school complex is rapidly deteriorating (see "abandoned classrooms", p. 112); the damage started with only three holes in the roof. St. George's Church (p. 87) has been replastered rather than restored.

The Straits Chinese Cheah Kongsi (p. 33) was re-roofed with imperial yellow tiles and polychromatic r.c. dragons. The Khoo Kongsi office building (p. 60) has had its turn-of-the-century interior gutted out in the course of renovations. As the Confucian principle of benevolence applied to clan or guild welfare fades from the trustees' memories, various Chinese clan associations and guilds are planning to privatise their historic properties to developers.

There is also good news. The restoration of the fabulous Cheong Fatt Tze Mansion (p.106) is nearing completion, the Protestant Cemetery (p. 130) has been cleaned and repaired, the Museum (p. 89) has been restored and will soon reopen - a new addition will be the Penang Heritage Trust gift shop in the converted hill railway carriage.

The federal government has allocated RM 3.5 million for the restoration of the Acheen Street Mosque and No 67 Acheen Street (p. 25), which will house a Haj Museum.

The recently launched American Express Heritage Trail, with brochures and signage, marks out a good walking tour of heritage sites from Fort Cornwallis down Jalan Mesjid Kapitan Keling (Pitt Street) into the Armenian Street-Acheen Street enclave.

The Armenian Street-Acheen Street enclave has long been identified as Penang's pilot heritage development area. The plans for its rehabilitation and pedestrianisation, as a first step towards realising Penang's possibilities as a heritage city, has been on the drawing board for years. Many local and international planners and conservationists have devoted their hopes and energies to it. The potential tourism benefits to Penang are obvious. Yet the political will and vision is still gravely lacking to carry out this urban regeneration project.

The second edition carries the following revisions. Several readers have pointed out to me that Frank Forster was acquitted on drug charges, not hung (p. 70). Shaikh Ghani of Madura was actually Abdul Ghani (p.25). Tengku Syed Hussain died some years before 1840, probably in 1829 (p. 27) and the author of *Kisah Pelayaran* (p. 165) was Ibrahim Munshi, not to be confused with Munshi Abdullah.

The Government House on Light Street (p. 108, p. 114) was built by Francis Light, not by Robert Farquhar. The author and other historians have been misled by F.G. Stevens who wrote in his *Early History of Prince of Wales Island* (JMBRAS, 1929):

> Another work of Mr. Farquhar's appears to have been the construction of Government House. This was a fine rectangular house with handsome reception rooms, lying about fifty yards from the north beach. It still forms part of the Convent buildings. It is shown in Mr. Purcell's map (1807-1808) and is mentioned in the survey records of 1807. It will be remembered that Sir George Leith complained of the fact that the most appropriate site for a Government House had become the property of Scott & Company. But it appears from a list of houses rented by the Honourable Company appended to one of Mr. Farquhar's reports that the Company in Farquhar's time paid a rent of 250 dollars a month for their Government House, besides having to keep the house in repair and to keep up the sea wall in front of it. And in the survey records of 1807 the site of the Government House is shown as Scott's land. The inference seems to be that the house was built by Scott & Company by arrangement with the Government, who must have obtained a long lease of it on the above conditions.

Despite Stevens' view, oral history has always maintained that the Government

House was Light's house. The Convent Light Street community remembers the well the next to the Government House as "Light's Well", although this was probably Light's private well rather than the Town Well sunk by him (see Leith's map of 1803).

Light's house appears in the Popham map of 1798 as the "Superintendent's" residence (Captain Francis Light was modestly titled "superintendent" while subsequent administrators were posted as "lieutenant governor" or "governor"), and the same cruciform footprint appears in Leith's map of 1803 as "Government House".

Similarly, Suffolk House was not, as was assumed by Stevens, built by W.E. Phillips, but by Light. The two properties are explicitly mentioned in Light's will of 1794, in which he bequeathed to Martina Rozells his "Garden house" and his "Bungaloe in George Town". Suffolk House was a Garden House - in 18th century Anglo-Indian terms, a country mansion - and not a garden shed, as

alleged by Stevens.

That Light was capable of erecting these two substantial brick structures is affirmed by the record that he had imported convict labour in 1789 for making bricks and building roads. We know that the massive Fort Cornwallis was rebuilt in brick in 1793.

That he did in fact build Suffolk House and the "Bungaloe in George Town" is supported by the account of *Brick Buildings on Prince of Wales Island 1793,* in which Light was mentioned as owning "2 Dwelling Houses & Offices" worth 16,000 Spanish Dollars.

Next on the list was James Scott with "1 Dwelling House & Office" worth 8,000 Spanish Dollars. The total worth of brick buildings on the island was valued at 88,650 Spanish Dollars - including many small shops and houses worth 1,000 or 2,000 Spanish Dollars each. This account is reproduced in *Penang Past and Present 1786-1963,* published by the City Council of George Town, Penang, in 1966.

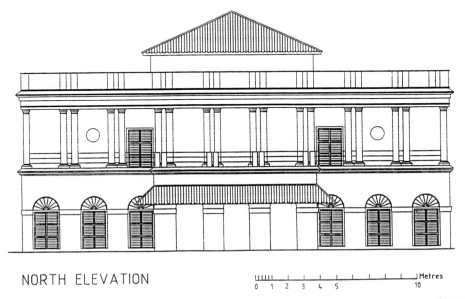

NORTH ELEVATION

Metres
0 1 2 3 4 5   10

Suffolk House as a Garden House c 1818 - based on 1993 dilapidation survey conducted by Bruce Pettman and Bob Terret, SACON Heritage Unit, South Australia

The above reassessment makes Suffolk House and the Government House, now dated 1790-93, the two oldest surviving British colonial buildings in Malaysia.

More about Light and Martina was uncovered this year by American novelist Susan Ellen Gross. She delved into the court cases where Martina tried to sue James Scott and other executors of the Light Estate for misappropriation. The judge John Dickens was hardly inclined to give the Eurasian widow her due in a court of law, biased as he was against various European settlers' "convenient women and their spurious offspring". Subsequent historians up to the 20th century have treated Martina no better, persistently denying her claim to the assets willed to her by Light.

Light the enterprising trader was no colonialist prototype like Raffles. Approaching the 200th anniversary of Light's death on 21st October 1994, it is perhaps time to rehabilitate the reputations of Light and Martina, and to give their building legacy a good chance of being conserved.

The Penang Heritage Trust is persevering in its efforts to restore Suffolk House before the Commonwealth Games of 1998, and to create an urban heritage park along the banks of the Air Itam River. A dilapidation survey of Suffolk House was carried out by Australian architects. The building was stabilized and a tent put over it to protect it from the elements. Many foreigners, but few locals, have come forward as generous sponsors and volunteers.

Sue Gross has also uncovered the mysterious identity of Martina Rozells - this will be revealed in a monograph soon to be published by the Penang Heritage Trust.

Meanwhile, Syed Mohamed Alatas (p. 35) has been identified as an Achehnese of Arab descent. The Syed Alatas Mansion at 128 Armenian Street has been restored with French technical assistance and is looking marvellous. Regretfully, the plan to use it as a heritage resource centre, initially agreed upon by the Municipal, State and Federal governments, has not been implemented.

Datuk Haji Fathil Basheer, the son of Sheikh Zacharia and the grandson of Sheikh Omar (p. 27) died on 4 October 1994 at the age of 95. He was a Justice of the Peace, the first secretary of the Muslim Religious Council and the founder of Kampung Melayu in Air Itam.

He did not live to see the opening of the Syed Alatas Mansion or the rehabilitation of the Armenian Street-Acheen Street enclave, although he had contributed more than anyone else to the historical knowledge of the area. He was the last living link to the noble and gracious old world of the Acheen Street community.

The author married the Mandailing nobleman Abdur-Razzaq Lubis, and is now called Khoo Salma Lubis. The couple are expecting their first baby. The two writers presently live and work in the recently restored shophouse, Dr. Sun Yat Sen's Base at 120 Armenian Street (p. 34), and are encouraging their friends to restore heritage houses and move back into the inner city.

5 October 1994

Postscript: When visiting Medan in 1994, we were told that I could not use my husband's clan name 'Lubis', but had to be installed into a suitable clan. A traditional wedding was held and I became a 'Nasution'. I am honoured to be part of the family of Dr. Rizali H. Nasution (Humaniora chairman, Badan Warisan Sumatra vice-chairman) and Drs. Z. Pangaduan Lubis, the foremost cultural authority on the Mandailings in Sumatra.

STREETS

OF GEORGE TOWN

PENANG

Text & Photographs by Khoo Su Nin
@ Khoo Salma Nasution

Where East meets West - coping of Kuan Yin See roof, Burmah Road.

Watching the changing world

PREFACE

When Francis Light established George Town in 1786, he sited it on a swampy, malaria-infested part of the island. The East India Company in Bengal considered Penang a dubious investment.

For the first half century, the fortunes of the settlement rose and fell according to the vagaries of the spice market, exacerbated by losses to rampant piracy in the Straits of Malacca.

As a British trading post, the port of Penang provided the East India Company a strategic base to challenge Dutch supremacy in the Straits and to further expand the trade with China.

Penang's founding was a personal dream for Light and a business opportunity for his partner James Scott.

For the Sultan of Kedah, the East India Company's presence was desired to counteract threats from Kedah's powerful neighbours, although the promise of protection was not honoured by Light's superiors. For the local traders, the free and neutral British port was preferable to the Dutch trading posts which imposed heavy restrictions and taxes, and to the native ports which offered little security from pirates or the monopolies of rival chieftains and princes.

But Penang was more than a port. The colony which Light created offered a liberal haven where each settler could establish the foundation for future generations.

This was true for the Malays escaping Siamese attacks in Kedah, the Eurasians fleeing religious persecution in South Thailand, the Chinese rejecting Manchu oppression to make their fortunes in the Nanyang and the South Indians leaving behind poverty and strife in their subcontinent.

It was also true for the Straits Chinese and Indian Muslim traders from Malacca and the coastal areas seeking new opportunities, the Burmese and Indians who followed their colonial employers to a new land, the Armenian, Persian and Jewish diaspora extending their trading chain east of India, as well as the Arabs and Acehnese moving in to consolidate their spice trade and to propagate Islam in the region.

In this crossroads of great civilizations, in a port where dozens of tongues were spoken, in a compact melting pot the size of George Town, a unique Straits culture evolved.

Over the last two centuries, Penang has meant many things to many people. Written records predominantly reflect the observations of travellers and the concerns of the public administration, or document the contributions of the wealthy.

A democratic way to relate Penang's past lives is to interpret the streets and historic buildings as physical evidence of the diverse peoples who have taken part in the city's growth.

Conservation efforts are urgently needed to allow this rich past to contribute to our future, because the streets of George Town, and the memory of these streets, belong to all the children of Penang.

ACKNOWLEDGEMENTS

The past has been brought to life for me by the elderly people I have met. Foremost is Dato' Haji Fathil Basheer, whose motto "Life is worth living as long as you can do something for your fellow man" has kept him going for almost a century. Born in 1899, his remarkable memory for the ancient stories of his youth makes him a living link to 19th century Penang.

My main source of information for local Chinese history and folk culture is Ong Seng Huat, a brilliant researcher and writer in the Mandarin language. We both have gained from older historians, both amateur and academic, who have sustained an interest in local history all these years when its importance was all but ignored.

Pioneering the study of cultural influences in the region's vernacular architecture is Frank Campbell of Deakin University, Australia, whose identification of the Anglo-Indian Garden Houses of Penang and the cross-synthesis of the Anglo-Indian and Malay building traditions contribute to the sections in this book on Suffolk House, Chulia Street and Kedah Road.

Among those who have done work on Penang's urban history are Dr. Jon Lim of National University of Singapore, who has conducted extensive research on the history of architects and architecture in the former Straits Settlements, and Dr. Goh Ban Lee of Universiti Sains Malaysia's Centre for Policy Research who in elucidating current realities has consistently referred to the history of town planning - I share his faith that our society can learn from its and others' past mistakes.

I am grateful to the Penang State Government and the Municipal Council of Penang Island for their encouraging support, and for giving priority to the heritage question; the State Museum & Art Gallery of Penang for assistance and permission to reproduce the early views of Penang; the Kedah State Museum for assistance; the Penang Heritage Trust and the Majlis Warisan Malaysia for their continuing support.

I am most thankful to the following individuals for reading through the text and providing valuable feedback - Mr. Amiruddin Fawzi, Dr. Choong Sim Poey, Ms. Patricia Tusa Fels, Dr. Ghulam Sarwar, Mr. Kamaruddin Hussain, Mr. Lim Hooi Siang, Mr. N. Meerah, Dr. Judith Nagata, Mrs. Mary Smith, Mr. P. Rajavelan (Krishna); Mr. Victor Tan for permission to reproduce his old postcards; others who have freely given of their knowledge and time; those who have kindly let me into their homes and associations and allowed me to take photographs; my parents and sister for their unquestioning support.

At this early stage, building plans, land records and probates are still buried in their archives, local and overseas libraries have yet to be combed. Some Chinese records, and most Arab, Jawi and Tamil records have yet to be sourced and translated, and generally these materials have yet to be made easily accessible to researchers and the interested public.

As history can and should always be responsibly revised, refined and enriched, I welcome corrections, additional information and alternative points of view.

NOTES

This guide surveys a selection of interesting streets in George Town up to the city limits and a little beyond to cover the early settlements of Batu Uban, Air Itam and Tanjung Tokong. As in colloquial use, "Penang" is at various times used to mean either Penang State, Penang Island or George Town.

A decision was made to use the prewar names of the streets, as these are more directly related to the urban development of George Town. The old street names and their contemporary equivalent are listed in an index.

Chinese street names are mostly given in Hokkien, reflecting the prevalent use of this dialect among the Penang Chinese, and the author's bias.

The commentaries are deliberately weighted to 18th and 19th century history, with occasional reference to the modern period. The intention is to establish a strong picture of George Town's foundation, assuming that the reader can easily refer to the common histories of the Straits Settlements and the Federated Malay States, and subsequently the history of Malaysia.

Rather than assail the reader with a plethora of names, dates and events, this guide concentrates on some colourful personalities, periods and themes, repeated from different perspectives.

The charm of George Town's streets is found in the intimate relationship between the monuments and the buildings of ordinary people. Early vernacular buildings are given some prominence, because they are yet not fully appreciated and are hence the most vulnerable. Their rarity has to be seen in the context not only of the state's but also of the country's built heritage stock.

Shophouse row, Kinta Lane

CONTENTS

Ceramic shard chien nien (cut and paste craft) gable decoration, Cheong Fatt Tze Mansion, Leith Street

The Standard Chartered Bank
India House
Gedung Aceh
Badjenid & Sons
Koe Guan Office

Bishop Street LEBUH BISHOP
San Wooi Wooi Koon

Brick Kiln Road JALAN BRICK KILN
The Diamond Jubilee Sikh Temple

Bridge Street JALAN C.Y. CHOY
The Temple of the City Protector

Burmah Lane LORONG BURMA
Dhammikarama Burmese Buddhist
Temple
Wat Chaiya Mangkalaram

Burmah Road JALAN BURMA
Loke Thye Kee
Kuan Yin See
Loh Leong San's Family Residence
Church of Immaculate Conception

Campbell Street LEBUH CAMPBELL
Campbell Street Market

Cannon Square MEDAN CANNON
Khoo Kongsi

Carnarvon Street LEBUH CARNARVON
Li Teik Seah Building
Seh Teoh Kongsi

Che Em Lane LORONG CHE EM

Cheapside CHEAPSIDE

China Street LEBUH CHINA
Cheng Ho Seah
Chettiar Lodge

China Street Ghaut GAT LEBUH CHINA
Wisma Kastam

Chowrasta Road JALAN CHOWRASTA

Chulia Street LEBUH CHULIA
Yen Keng Hotel
Japanese Club
Nagore Shrine
Noordin Family Tomb
Penang Teochew Association
Yeoh Kongsi
Central Fire Station
United Association of Cantonese
Districts

Church Street LEBUH GEREJA
Chung Keng Kwee Ancestral Hall,
Hai Kee Chan, Office & Residence

Cintra Street LEBUH CINTRA

College Square MEDAN MAKTAB

Dato Kramat Road
JALAN DATO KERAMAT

Haji Kassim Mosque
Brown Memorial
Datuk Keramat Smelting
Penang Hindu Sabah

Downing Street LEBUH DOWNING

Drury Lane LORONG DRURY

Esplanade Road
JALAN PADANG KOTA LAMA

Farquhar Street LEBUH FARQUHAR
St. George's Church
Francis Light Memorial
Penang State Museum
The Eastern & Oriental Hotel
Cathedral of the Assumption

Glugor Road JALAN SULTAN AZLAN SHAH
Batu Uban Mosque

Green Lane JALAN MESJID NEGERI

Gurney Drive PESIARAN GURNEY

Hutton Lane LORONG HUTTON

Jelutong Road JALAN JELUTONG
Khie Heng Bee Mills
Huttenbach Godowns
Syed Sheikh Al-Hadi's Residence
Mesjid Maqbul

Detail, Love Lane shophouse

Kampong Deli KAMPONG DELI
Kampong Kolam KAMPONG KOLAM
   Kapitan Kling's Tomb
Kampong Malabar KAMPONG MALABAR
Katz Street LEBUH KATZ
Kedah Road JALAN KEDAH
   Hidayathul Muslim Association
Kelawai Road JALAN KELAWAI
   Jimmy Boyle's House
Kimberley Street LEBUH KIMBERLEY
King Edward Place
PESARA KING EDWARD
   Victoria Memorial Clock Tower
King Street LEBUH KING
   Chong San Wooi Koon
   Tua Pek Kong Temple
   Toi San Nin Yong Hui Kwon
    & Wu Ti Meow
   Ng See Kah Meow
   Tseng Lung Fui Kon
   Kar Yin Fooi Koon
   Lee Sih Chong Soo
   Chin Si Tong Soo
   Poe Choo Seah
   Former Ho Seng Society Base
   Ku Chen Hooi
Larut Road JALAN LARUT
   Limburg
   The Wesley Methodist Church
Leith Street LEBUH LEITH
   Cheong Fatt Tze Mansion
Leith Street Ghaut GAT LEBUH LEITH

Light Street LEBUH LIGHT
   Fort Cornwallis
   Seri Rambai
   Foo Tye Sin's Mansion
   Koh Seang Tat's Fountain
   The State Assembly Buildings
   The Convent Light Street
   The Government House
   Supreme Court Building
   Logan Memorial
Love Lane LORONG LOVE
   Sun Tak Association
   Carpenters' Guild
Lumut Lane LORONG LUMUT
   Sheikh Zachariah Basheer & Sons
Macalister Road JALAN MACALISTER
   The Baobab Tree
   Philomatic Society
Madras Lane LORONG MADRAS
   Hu Yew Seah
Magazine Road JALAN MAGAZINE
   Hui Aun Kong Hooi
Malay Street LEBUH MELAYU
Market Street LEBUH PASAR
Muntri Street LEBUH MUNTRI
   The Goldsmith's Association
   The Hailam Association & Temple
   King Wan Association
Northam Road JALAN SULTAN AHMAD SHAH
   The Protestant Cemetery
   Runnymede
   Shih Chung School
   Hardwicke
   Soonstead
   Asdang House
   The Aloes
   Woodville
   Leong Yin Kean Mansion
   Homestead
Pangkor Road JALAN PANGKOR
Peel Avenue LEBUHRAYA PEEL
Penang Road JALAN PENANG
   Seh Ong Kongsi
   Wing Look Restaurant
   St. Xavier's Church

Detail, upper Beach Street

Detail, lower Beach Street

INTRODUCTION

When Western ships first sailed through the Straits of Malacca, Penang was part of the Kingdom of Kedah. The island was locally known as *Pulau Kesatu,* and also as *Pulo Pinang* to voyagers since Admiral Cheng Ho in the early 15th century because Tamils came to trade in *pinang* (areca nut).

The Portuguese, who stopped at *Batu Feringgi* (Foreigner's Rock) to refill their ships with fresh water on the way to Malacca, noted *Pulo Pinaom* on their maps.

When Light planted the British flag on the island in August 1786, he named it the "Prince of Wales Island". Penang then became part of India.

The settlement to be built on the northeastern cape was named "George Town", after George III. The cape was formerly known as *Tanjong Penaigre* because of the hardy ironwood trees called *penaga,* which

Light induced the original inhabitants and early settlers to clear by firing a cannon full of coins into the forest. Locals still refer to George Town as *Tanjung.*

In early Penang, regional traders brought pepper, clove, nutmeg, gambier, ivory and other produce of the archipelago to be sold to European, American, Arab, Indian and Chinese ships. Areca nut, bird's nest and small quantities of tin were mainly exported to the China market. The British traded woollens, chintzes and opium for spices.

The following is an outline of ensuing events: In 1800, a strip of land on the other side of the North Channel was acquired for the security of the port; it was named Province Wellesley. In 1805, Penang was elevated to the status of India's fourth Presidency.

In 1819, Raffles founded Singapore, and the Penang settlement was left to flounder. In 1826, Penang, Malacca and Singapore were incorporated to form the Straits Settle-

---

The port of Penang - trading offices and godowns near Weld Quay

ments with the seat of government in Penang; by this time, the port of Singapore had overtaken Penang in importance, and in 1832 the capital of the Straits Settlements was transferred to Singapore.

In the mid-19th century, a rise in the world tin market created a "tin rush" of Chinese coolies into the Malay states of Perak and Selangor. In 1867, the control of the Straits Settlements was transferred from India to the Colonial Office in Singapore, and then the Suez Canal was opened two years later, speeding Penang's recovery.

After the Pangkor Treaty of 1874, increasing British intervention allowed the agriculture and tin potential of the Malay States to be further exploited. Penang now flourished as the export centre for this northern hinterland, especially after the development of the Federated Malay States Railway.

The age of the steamship, followed by that of the telegraph, facilitated the swift transmission of information, revolutionised trade and commerce, and allowed the Straits Settlements society to keep up with Western fashions. At the turn of the century, the regional trade had expanded enough to encourage the leading European companies in Singapore to establish branches in Penang.

The golden age of Penang was ushered in by the tin, rubber and shipping industries. In those days, Medan, South Thailand and Rangoon looked to Penang as a provincial capital - which in turn looked to Singapore as the metropolis. Commodity crashes devastated some families in the late 1920s and 30s, and more fortunes were lost in the Second World War.

Bombs were dropped on the city, and Penang was occupied by the Japanese from December 1941 until September 1945.

The end of the war was followed by recon-

Beach Street at the turn of the century

struction and a general pre-occupation with fighting Communism.

In the 1950s, the election of City Councillors was introduced. On 1st January 1957, George Town was given City status, on the centenary of the formation of the first Municipal Council of George Town. The population then stood at 234,855.

When Malaysia attained Independence in August that year, Penang joined the new country as a State.

Today, George Town is the commercial centre for Penang State, West Malaysia's northern states and the Indonesia-Malaysia-Thailand Growth Triangle. The state of Penang has about 1.3 million inhabitants - almost equally divided between island and mainland - and over three million tourists a year.

HISTORIC COMMUNITIES

At the time he founded Penang, Light was no stranger to the Malay-speaking world. The Englishman had been trading in the region since 1772, together with his life partner Martina Rozells, a local Eurasian of Portuguese descent. He was fluent in Malay and had befriended not only the Kedah court but also the heads of the local communities.

The leaders of the Malay, Tamil Muslim, Arab, Straits Chinese and Eurasian communities from Phuket, Aceh, Malacca and the Kedah coast who settled on the island during Light's lifetime can be considered Penang's pioneer settlers.

In the early years, the Malays from Kedah made up the largest group; they cleared the land and settled in the interior.

Apart from these, there were the Europeans, Arabs, Armenians, Jews, Burmese, Thais; Bugis, Ambonese, Javanese, Acehnese, Rawanese, Minangkabaus and other peoples of the archipelago; Tamils, Malabaris and other South Indian groups; Gujeratis, Bengalis, Parsis and other North Indian groups; Cantonese, Hokkiens, Hakkas, Teochews, Hainanese and other South Chinese groups; and later there were Ceylonese, Sikhs, Japanese, Filipinos, etc.

All these groups were active participants in the creation of a cosmopolitan city. Even today, Penang is distinguished by the many ethnic minorities and historic communities which add to the richness of West Malaysia's mainstream "Malay, Chinese and Indian" cultures.

The founding settlers evolved to be the core of the early permanent community. Two special groups which are closely identified with Penang are the *Peranakan Jawi* and the Straits Chinese, both urban elites and

An elegant Malay Eclectic house along Macalister Road (demolished).

cultural hybrids which were relatively more receptive to European influence than their contemporaries. They are introduced here to provide an insight into the rich, complex and as yet little understood Straits subcultures which have played a prominent role in Penang's unique development.

The Indian Muslims formed the most important business community in Penang during the first fifty years. The main group consisted of Tamil Muslims who were also called *Keling* or *Chulia*.

Wherever they settled in the Straits of Malacca, the traders took local wives, and their descendants were called *Peranakan Jawi,* denoting Straits-born Muslims*,* or *Jawi Pekan,* which meant "Town Malays".

Indian Muslim communities were well-established in 17th century Aceh, 15th century Malacca and in Kedah sometime before, having married into the top echelons of those societies. For the most part, the leading Indian Muslims and their descendants comprised the Muslim urban elite in Penang.

In their role as leaders of the wider Muslim community, they endowed waqf, built mosques and Malay vernacular schools. Being well-educated, well-travelled and open to both European and Arab influences, they contributed to Malay literature and publishing. The same was also true of the Arabs, who were fewer in numbers but enjoyed more prestige in the local society.

In Penang's early years, the most important regional traffic was the pepper and spice trade with Aceh, dominated by Indian Muslim and Arab merchants. In the 1870s, the Dutch sieged Aceh and embargoed all Muslim traders, the latter being potential Acehnese sympathisers. The cream of the Indian Muslim commercial class declined rapidly, just at the time when the Chinese began to arrive in large numbers to work the tin mines, and Hindus from Southern India were being widely recruited as plantation labourers.

By the 1930s, the term *"Peranakan Jawi"* was dropped, as most people of Indian Muslim descent who had come to identify themselves with the Malay majority, now call themselves Malays. Today, the Indian Muslim / *Peranakan Jawi* / Malay community in Malaysia, and especially in Penang, form a social continuum - hence the rich historic connotations of the term "Penang Malay".

Before Penang, Chinese settlements in the *Nanyang* (South Seas) thrived not only in 15th century Malacca but also in north Java, South Thailand and the Kedah coast. In the beginning, male traders took wives, who might have been Batak, Thai or Burmese. Subsequent generations of

Three-storey elite shophouse along King Street. The house has two sections - a major house and a minor house - sharing a common courtyard (endangered).

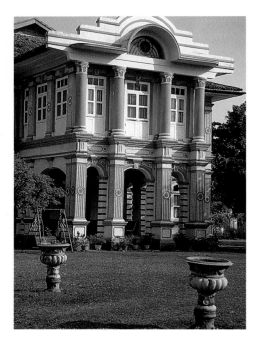

migrants, they expanded their numbers by encouraging the chain migration of relatives from their clan villages in China, organised with the support of clan associations.

Eventually, the Straits Chinese minority came to ally itself with the Straits government, sending their children for western education. The group evolved into a western-educated elite, with advantages to obtaining lucrative government farms.

By the turn of the century, the men had adopted western attire, while the women creatively modified their own local fashions. The Straits Chinese came to be identified by social-economic class, political orientation, gentrified lifestyle and an eclectic taste for the finest things from all cultures. While not all those born in the Straits could apply, the Chinese who attained enough wealth could claim to be Straits Chinese by association and by assimilation.

The Baba Nyonya in Penang came to speak a distinctive Hokkien *patois* incorporating Malay words; so do their counterpart communities in Medan, Phuket and Rangoon. In contrast, the southern Baba Nyonya of Malacca (and by extension of Singapore) speak a Malay *patois* with Hokkien words.

Today, the Straits Chinese have become more or less integrated into the general Chinese community, although the former were more likely to be English-educated and Anglicized in outlook, while the latter were more likely to be Chinese-educated and influenced by Chinese nationalism. In Penang, Malacca and Singapore, the recent generations of Straits Chinese have become westernised, not only in form, but also in spirit - many have even emigrated to English-speaking countries.

womenfolk retained many elements of the indigenious lifestyle.

Their descendants became known as Baba Nyonya, Straits-born Chinese or Straits Chinese, as the communities were later concentrated in the urban areas of the Straits Settlements. Further down the line, the Straits Chinese intermarried among their own kind; occasionally the daughters were married off to the best specimens of the male *sinkeh* (recent immigrants from China).

The early Straits Chinese were fluent in Malay, the *lingua franca* of the Straits trading world. Compared to other Chinese traders, the Straits Chinese had an advantage in the real estate opportunities and regional trade, relying on their established ties with the archipelago trading community.

When their dominance in Penang society was challenged by later waves of Chinese

Straits Chinese Art Deco Eclectic, Anson Road

Incidentally, it is the manifestations of Straits Chinese material culture, especially of their Golden Age in the 1920s - the mansions and lavish interiors, the refined Nyonya ware and the food served on them, the romantic dress and jewellery - which generally inspire nostalgia for "prewar Penang".

URBAN DEVELOPMENT

At the start Light assigned streets in the commercial town to the Eurasian, Chinese and Indian Muslim communities. The Malays settled in a "Malay Town" on the southern fringe, soon consolidated by Tengku Syed Hussain from Aceh.

Although the Europeans reserved North Beach for themselves, George Town never experienced the formal segregation that was created in Singapore, or to an even greater extent in colonial port cities like Hong Kong and Yokohama.

The reason for this, besides Light's own alliance with the Asian communities, was a weak and inadequately funded administration in George Town's formative years. The Europeans were always in a very small minority, even after taking into consideration the Eurasian community, who socially and geographically acted as a buffer group between the former and the overwhelming non-European population.

To provide a frame of reference, George Town began with a historic centre at the tip of the cape. Arterial roads radiated along the north and east coasts, and to the hills in the interior.

Before he died in 1794, Light had laid out a gridiron of streets bordered by Light Street, Beach Street, Chulia Street and Pitt Street. Beyond this gridiron, the network of streets developed in a sprawling fashion, with mostly informal housing and unclear land ownership, until the Municipal authorities took up serious town planning and urban renewal almost a century later.

Each stage of expansion required the recovery of swamp land. In the early 19th century, the town spread naturally towards the Prangin Creek and the Bound Ditch (now Transfer Road). This area, intensively built up with double-storey shophouses, roughly constitutes today's "Inner City". In the mid-19th century, the town was bounded by Larut Road, Anson Road, Seang Tek Road and Magazine Road. Most of the early permanent shophouses in the inner city date from this period. Some had internal wells but most had no back lanes - the latter were only created with alterations at the turn of the century.

Leading Chinese traders lived in elite shophouses until the

Shophouse row, Phee Choon Road

turn of the 20th century, when they began to move out into the suburbs. There are also many 19th century ensembles comprising primarily residential rowhouses built by clan associations or by patriarchs for their kin.

In the late 19th century, the town limits were Cantonment Road, Scotland Road and the Pinang River, incorporating extensive residential suburbs. Weld Quay was reclaimed.

In this period of affluence which lasted until the early 20th century, well-constructed bungalows with gardens mushroomed in the fringe, while the earlier wooden shophouses and *kampung* houses in the compact town centre were rebuilt as brick shophouses. Most of Penang's aesthetically appealing architecture dates from this era.

The prime commercial area of Beach Street saw many new developments. Apart from that, most brick shophouses in the historic centre from the early and mid-19th century were likely to be retained although in some cases they were given new facades.

The present boundaries of George Town were demarcated to border on Tanjung Tokong, Waterfall Road, Boundary Road, Green Lane, Free School Road and Perak Road.

With the economic and population boom in the early 20th century, commercially rentable terrace houses were developed as a form of property investment.

All prewar rented properties came under the Control of Rent Act (1966) which explains not only the widespread survival of shophouse ensembles in George Town, but also the original condition or dilapidation of these buildings. The Rent Control Act was repealed in September 1997, taking full effect by the turn of the millennium.

ARCHITECTURE

Socially and architecturally, Penang was the point at which the Anglo-Indian empire encountered the Chinese civilization in the Nusantara. Diverse building traditions were adapted to the wet tropical climate, incorporating indigenious building forms and materials.

Francis Light imported Indian and Chinese brick-layers, and bricks were made in the Company's kilns. After 1789, Penang became a penal settlement for India, and convict labour from Bengal constructed all the government buildings and roads.

The earliest structures were erected in *nibong* palm by local Malays, but subsequently Chinese or Indian builders were employed for the more substantial masonry buildings. In the first quarter of the 19th

Corner building, Leith Street

century, terra cotta tiles began to be used, and these gradually replaced attap as the main roofing material in the urban areas.

George Town has the region's largest pool of prewar buildings and a reasonably intact historic centre. Among the Malaysian states, Penang alone has an impressive collection of early 19th century Anglo-Indian buildings; from this point, British Indian architectural influences were disseminated to the rest of the Straits of Malacca.

Penang also boasts a unique range of 19th century South Indian Muslim architecture, which includes mosques, shrines and domestic buildings.

Among the cities outside China, Penang is a showcase of Southern Chinese shophouse and temple architecture, featuring varying degrees of local and European influences. From the mid-19th century until the 1910s, Penang offered great opportunities for Chinese craftsmanship at a time when China was in political upheaval. The Cantonese built their district associations and the Hokkiens built their clan associations - institutions which played important roles during the years of large-scale immigration.

In the late 19th century, the various historic building traditions that had taken root in Penang were synthesised into the predominant local styles. The Europeans being more restrained limited themselves to adapting Anglo-Indian buildings to tropical Malay forms, creating the "colonial bungalow".

Penang's domestic architecture overwhelmingly expresses the tastes of the culturally hybrid Straits Chinese and Jawi Peranakan. These permanent communities were relatively affluent, had extensive families and long-term interests in the settlement, in contrast to the large transient population of single male immigrants.

Seeking to distinguish themselves from the new migrants and their more functional material culture, the established classes intensified their tastes for the ornate, providing a market for Straits Eclectic style architecture which romantically combined East-

Making way for the Komtar development.

ern and Western elements and alluded freely to both ethnic and Classical idioms. Inspired by the plaster arabesques of Indian Empire architecture, the Straits Chinese switched from ceramic shard work to florid stucco decoration at the turn of the century.

The Jawi Peranakan merchants built the early Straits Eclectic bungalows in the mid-19th century, followed by the Straits Chinese elite. The latter only gave up shophouse living late in the 19th century, but by the early 20th century, their ostentatious villas in the suburbs were unmatched in luxury and ornamental splendour. Around the same time, the emerging Straits middle-class, like their Victorian counterparts, moved into quality terrace housing developments.

The traditional Malay house continued to develop, incorporating foreign elements such as Georgian fanlights and louvred windows, masonry basements and stairs, and the hip-and-gable roof.

European architectural firms and building plans made their appearance at the turn of the century. The largest practices were based in Singapore, with branches in Penang. By the 1910s the first Western-trained local architects had begun their prolific careers.

Their tradition of eclecticism, which had started to evolve a truly Malaysian identity in contemporary architecture, was regrettably curtailed after the last war, with the introduction of the International Style which had no reference to existing vernaculars, either in form, scale or construction.

STREET CULTURE

The names of streets trace the city's development and remember the historic communities. Certain streets were named after leading landowners and local administrators; other street names were commonplace throughout the former British empire - King Street, Victoria Street, Campbell Street.

Local place names, in contrast, were more likely to commemorate economic activities and landmarks.

Almost every ethnic group in George Town (including bygone communities) is remembered by a street name - Malay Street, Patani Road, Singgora Lane, Acheen Street, Kampong Deli, Bertam Lane, Kampong Java, Bangkok Lane, Thaton Lane, Trang Road, Siam Road, Burmah Road, Chulia Street, Kampong Malabar, Tamil Street, China Street, Hong Kong Road, Amoy Lane, Swatow Lane, Cintra Street, Yahudi Road, Armenian Street, Ceylon Lane and more.

Diverse peoples from all over the world contributed to what makes Penang different today - the cosmopolitan culture, the architecture, the festivals, the food.

Hanging out at the corner coffeeshop - a way of life in traditional neighbourhoods.

emporium of things from all over the world, many of which are finding their way into the antique shops today - English porcelain dolls, Italian mirrors, German wall clocks, Japanese cameras, etc.

Even before the age of the telegraph, the Penang community kept abreast of happenings in other parts of the world, through extensive family and trade ties throughout the Straits of Malacca, China, India, Arabia and Europe.

Penangites abroad nostalgically refer to George Town as their *kampung* - their overgrown village. George Town is in fact a collection of urban villages and traditional neighbourhoods. The history of the city's growth includes the individual stories of how each historic community came to make its home in Penang.

After Singapore became the capital of the Straits Settlements in 1832, until British intervention in the Malay States in 1874, the colonial authorities paid little heed to Penang. Apart from the studies on secret societies, this chapter of Penang history has been the least written about.

However, far from being the "dark ages" of Penang, the mid-19th century was the period when the non-European communities consolidated their trading interests and established their territories within George Town. This was also the era of the greatest cultural fusion among the various ethnic groups that comprised the permanent community.

The cosmopolitan outlook is part of the heritage of a trading society. Penang is an

Various ethnic groups influenced each other, while being influenced by developments in their source countries.

The material culture and architecture of each historic community expressed claims of assimilation - through identification with the local society - and at the same time statements of difference - through reference to cultural origin.

Within the multi-ethnic society, cultural identity was popularly and conspicuously asserted through religious street festivals - Boria, flag processions, the Chingay Parade, the Nine Emperor Gods Festival, the Hungry Ghosts Festival, Thaipusam and so forth.

Even today, festivals in and through the streets of George Town are held the year round. The festivals have mainly departed from the versions in their source country, retaining much of the 19th century rituals while developing uniquely Malaysian elements.

Itinerant produce-sellers at Burmah Road

borne on shoulder yokes - a former example was *Nasi Kandar,* which is now permanently stationed in coffee shops.

Coffee shops, some purpose-built as corner lots, were places to read the newspapers, engage in popular debate or just sit and watch the world go by. The coffeeshop, the sundry shop, the Mamak stall, the wet market, the hawkers - all these continue to contribute to street life in the traditional neighbourhoods.

The inner city still has thriving residential pockets, the communities that keep Penang's traditions and festivals alive. Children still take the trishaw to school, look forward to the ice-cream man's visits and play in the five-foot ways.

Public interaction was encouraged by the arcaded five-foot ways - a municipally regulated act of consideration which provided shade for pedestrians. These semi-public areas allowed neighbours to sit around and chat, while they looked out for itinerant hawkers to bring their tid-bits.

The intrinsic value of the Straits shophouse ensembles has been recognized and well-appreciated by planners and urban designers. Suited to the local climate and highly adaptable in use and appearance, they combine residential and commercial functions in an economical and socially sensible manner, and contribute to healthy and varied neighbourhood patterns.

The shophouse city, of which George Town is the best example in the region, fostered the trading culture of the port city. The adaptability of the shophouse to changing times is the key to preserving the resilience of traditional business communities - wherein lies an essential part of the future of Penang.

Penang is also famous for its street hawkers. One can find good, freshly-cooked food around the clock. Hawker food flourished in the 19th century Penang society which largely comprised single men. Practically every hawker food has a story of the people who made it and the type of people who consumed it - *Kelinga Mee,* Chinese noodles cooked Indian style, originally catered to the tastes of port workers.

Then, as now, people had a wide variety to choose from. Foods from all over the world were mixed up in the proverbial melting pot, according to availability of ingredients and the evolving tastes of consumers.

Although now a more sedentary practice, street hawking grew out of the tradition of itinerant pedlars, who sold a range of wares from cloth to crockery. The goods were mostly

Chingay procession on Christmas day, Chulia Street

THE STREETS
in Alphabetical Order

The Thaipusam procession of the silver chariot drawn down Western Road. Whole coconuts are smashed on the road by devotees, as an offering to cleanse the Lord Murugan's path.

nese. It was the first Malay modern theatre to employ the proscenium stage and painted backdrops, and subsequently had a great influence on Malaysia's early film industry.

The Malays call this street *Lorong Pushi* as it was the address of the *Towkay Wayang*.

ACHEEN STREET

The earliest Arab urban community in Penang flourished around Acheen Street, immediately south of the grid planned by Francis Light.

During the first century of Penang's existence, the bulk of regional trade was conducted with Aceh in northern Sumatra. Aceh became the centre of the spice trade after Malacca came under Dutch rule, but the "pepper ports" were often troubled by feuding chieftains.

ABOO SITI LANE

Aboo Siti, also known as *Mamak Pushi,* is regarded as the father of *Bangsawan*, a form of Malay opera which originated in Penang in the 1870s.

A travelling troupe from Bombay brought *Wayang Parsi,* which was popular in India at the time. It so enthralled local audiences that Aboo Siti started a local company called *Kumpulan Pusi Indera-Bangsawan* in the 1890s, which toured Malaya and Indonesia.

The name *Bangsawan*, meaning "nobility", was apparently bestowed by Tunku Kudin (see also Udini Road). The cast was usually courtly, with attendant characters and jesters.

Bangsawan was incredibly popular, not only with Malay audiences, but also with Indians and the Malay-speaking Straits Chi-

Penang offered a protected harbour where spices brought by Malay, Acehnese, Indian Muslim and Arab traders from northern Sumatra could be resold to European and Chinese vessels.

By the 18th century, Aceh was already settled by Arab and Indian Muslim traders who made it the focal point for the spread of Islam throughout the archipelago. One of these Arab traders was Tengku Syed Hussain Al-Aidid, a member of the Acehnese royal house and a rival to the monarch.

In 1792, Syed Hussain and his clan moved to Penang. He set up his office and godown on the waterfront at the end of Acheen Street (see also Beach Street) and founded the mosque of the Acheen Street community. Francis Light considered him "one of the wealthiest men on the island".

Mak Minah, the late Queen of Bangsawan

In Light's assessment of brick buildings on the island in 1793, Syed Hussain was named as the owner of a dwelling house-cum-office worth 6,000 Spanish Dollars - in this he was surpassed only by Light himself and his partner James Scott.

In 1814, at the invitation of Acehnese chieftains, Syed Hussain sent his son with a fleet of armed ships to take over the Acehnese throne. Saif-Al-Alam ruled as Sultan of Aceh until the British backed the old Sultan to recover his throne from the usurper in 1820.

The mosque is concealed from Acheen Street by a row of timber shophouses. This 19th century layout, providing only a narrow entrance to the mosque compound, is not unlike those of the neighbouring clan associations.

The bungalows around the mosque are survivors from the 19th century Arab *kampong*. These half-masonry half-timber buildings are among the earliest urban dwellings of the Muslim community.

On the west end of Acheen Street, around the playground, were two villages. The first was called *Kampong Che Long,* after a leader of the *Bendera Merah* (Red Flag)

secret society. Che Long was one of the principal instigators of the Penang Riots of 1867 (see also Armenian Street).

The second village was called *Kampong Tuan Guru,* after the highly influential 19th century religious teacher, Abdul Ghani from Madura. At least two mosques seem to have been inspired by him, the *Mesjid Tuan Guru* in Tanjung Tokong and one in Jelutong now known as *Mesjid Maqbul.*

Then in 1916, the *Madrasatul Al-Qur'an,* predecessor of the famous *Sekolah Al-Mashoor,* was started in *Kampong Tuan*

Above, houses in the mosque compound, No. 67 and No. 69 Acheen Street, which used to belong to the Basheer family. Below, the Acheen Street mosque's distinctive octagonal minaret, since restored.

Guru by a group of influential Arabs. The first teacher of the Islamic school in 1910 was Syed Abdul Rahman Al-Habshee from Java. Another personality who made his mark here was the theologian and astrologer Sheikh Tahir Jalaluddin, father of the present Governor of Penang.

Penang was the birth place of *Boria*, a popular tradition among the Acheen Street community. *Boria* was a form of entertainment which combined song, dance and satirical sketches - staged and participated by the ordinary folk. It was later frowned upon by the Islamic reformists as a Malay adaptation of the Indian Muharram festival.

During the ten-day Awal Muharram celebrations, wandering minstrels went from house to house performing *Boria*. The Red Flag and White Flag members often took swipes at each other during *Boria* competitions, and these often ended up in street brawls on the last day of Muharram. One old *Boria* verse goes like this:

Kampong Che Long, Khian Teik Kongsi,
Taukeh Ghee Hin sudah mati,
Tiada tiru, sendiri reka,
Kampong Che Long, Kompani kita.

(Roughly translated: "Che Long's Village, Khian Teik Society / The head of Ghee Hin Society is dead / We do not imitate others, we are original / Che Long's village, our own Company").

The Acheen Street community closely followed the events of the larger Muslim world. The issues of Acehnese independence and Turkish nationalism were debated in the coffeeshops.

Activist groups were formed and donations collected to support the causes of the Muslim brotherhood in other countries, at the same time when their Chinese associates were actively supporting the Republican Revolution in China (see also Armenian Street).

Acheen Street also became known as the "Second Jeddah". Pilgrims from all over the country, and from as far as Sumatra and Thailand, gathered in Penang to await the ship to Jeddah.

The mosque was a centre of prayer and religious discourse which prepared the pilgrims for their important mission.

The area thrived with the activities of pilgrim brokers, ticketing agencies, hotels, shops and printing presses which published most of the northern region's Islamic literature. This bazaar died out with the advent of the aeroplane - when the *kapal haji* was replaced by the *kapal terbang*, and the *Sheikh Haji* by the *Tabung Haji*.

The Chinese know this street as *Pak Cheok Kay* (Stone Workers' Street) because of the Chinese stone-workers here who carve

Acheen Street, still the centre for Islamic printing presses and bookstores.

pestles and mortars, in addition to Chinese and Muslim tombstones.

ACHEEN STREET MOSQUE

The *Mesjid Melayu* (Malay Mosque) or *Mesjid Jamek* (Friday Mosque), was founded in 1808 by Tengku Syed Hussain Al-Aidid.

The mosque and octagonal minaret are reminiscent of venacular mosques found in the archipelago. The mosque has a tiered roof with Chinese swallow ridges, and the structure is supported by rows of octagonal columns. The squarish mosque is surrounded by a low stone bench with an ancient well on the eastern side. The arcaded nothern façade was only added in the early 1900s.

Syed Hussain died in 1826 at a ripe old age and was buried beside the mosque, as is customary of mosque founders. The family burial ground is enclosed in a timber structure embellished with Qur'anic phrases. The surrounding cemetery also has a number of intricately carved Acehnese gravestones.

SHEIKH OMAR'S RESIDENCE

Sheikh Omar Basheer, the *imam* of the Acheen Street Mosque, resided at 69 Acheen Street (see also Sheikh Omar's Mausoleum, Ayer Itam).

The Commission which investigated the Penang Riots of 1867 required Muslim suspects to swear before Sheikh Omar that they were not secret society members.

In 1888, Sheikh Omar's son Haji Yahya opened the first Muslim registrar's office in this building. Another son, Sheikh Zachariah, became Mufti of Penang. Sheikh Zachariah permitted his house at 67 Acheen Street to be used by the *Madrasatul Al-Qur'an* in 1917 and when he died in 1926, left it as waqf for his four grandsons, the sons of Syed Ahmad Almashor.

GOH SAY ENG'S BUSINESS PREMISES

Goh Say Eng was one of the most influential of Dr. Sun Yat Sen's Penang supporters (see also Armenian Street). He sold his family properties one by one to support the 1911 Republican Revolution of China until he was left in dire poverty in his old age.

He was the founding chairman of the Tung Meng Hooi, Penang Branch in 1906 as well as the Penang Philomatic Society in 1908. Together with Dr. Sun Yat Sen, he started the Chinese paper Kwong Wah Jit Poh in 1910 to raise the awareness of the Chinese-reading public on current affairs. The Kwong Wah has survived as the longest-running newspaper in the country.

Say Eng's own elite townhouse (see also China Street) became the Reading Club of the Philomatic Union in the 1910s.

Goh Say Eng's elite shophouse which became the Philomatic Union's Reading Club.

AL-MADRASAH AL-MAHMOODIYAH AL-ARABIA

Popularly known as Madrasah Hamid Arabi, the former religious school and boarding house was founded around 1900 by Shaikh Abdul Hamid Al-Khahirah, an Indian Muslim diamond merchant. Shaikh Abdul Hamid and his son, who were educated in Cairo and India, taught the Arabic language, the Qur'an and Islamic law. Supported by donations from Muslim merchants, the school grew into an important institution in the 1920s when it had more than 200 students.

AH QUEE STREET

The street is named after Kapitan Chung Keng Kwee, who donated his terrace house fronting Beach Street to the Municipality for vehicular access. The Malays call it *Lorong Takia* because of the former *kampong* that was there before the street was created at the turn of the century. This street provides a long vista of the Capitan Kling Mosque minaret.

KEW LONG TONG LIM KONGSI

The "Hall of Nine Dragons" commemorates a venerated ancestor of the Lim clan, whose nine sons became chief magistrates of nine states throughout China during the Tang dynasty. Several Lim families were similarly influential in 20th century Penang.

The temple dates from the 1860s but has been renovated several times.

At the entrance is an old shrine to Mar Chor Poh, patron saint of seafarers, whose surname was Lim. The Lim Kongsi is the only local clan association with a female patron deity.

Above, the Madrasah's Straits Indian Eclectic facade. Below, possibly Penang's longest terrace house, with six sections and five airwells.

ANSON ROAD

Colonel (later Major-General) Archibald E.H. Anson was the last Lieutenant-Governor of Penang, from 1867, the year of the Penang Riots, until 1882, after which the office of the Resident Councillor was instituted. In a map of 1877, Anson Road formed a boundary of the Municipality.

Anson Road is lined with many old bungalows, some which have been sensibly adapted to new uses.

The Club Oriental was formerly the Penang Rubber Trade Association, where the Penang Rubber Exchange was conducted before the war. The mansion opposite is a stock-broker's office.

THE PENANG BUDDHIST ASSOCIATION

The association was founded in 1925 by a group of Straits Chinese Buddhists who wanted to study Buddhism untainted by the Taoist beliefs and superstitions commonly found in Chinese Buddhism.

Built in 1931, the Penang Buddhist Association is a wonderful example of a late Straits Eclectic-style temple. The interior is lavishly furnished with cast iron staircases,

The Straits Eclectic Buddhist temple and garden with miniature pagoda. Below, Ch'ng Teong Swee's Mansion on Anson Road, featuring highly artistic stucco work (now completely defaced).

large mother-of-pearl inlaid blackwood altar tables, multi-tiered chandeliers and lotus-flower patterned floor tiles.

On Wesak Day, hundreds of Buddhist devotees dressed in white assemble here for an evening processsion. The temple follows the Mahayana Pure Land Sect but also encourages teachings of the Theravada School.

The association derives income from a residential estate developed in the 1930s. It is dissected by roads with Buddhist names like Dharma, Deva Pada, Bodhi and Nirvana, which are lined with Straits Eclectic Art Deco terrace houses.

ARGUS LANE

The early Eurasian Catholic community lived around the Cathedral of the Assumption in a *kampung* of bungalows. One of these buildings was *Argus House,* where Penang's first independent newspaper, the *Pinang Argus,* was published from 1867 to 1873. The last of these early dwellings survives at the back of the Cathedral.

ARMENIAN STREET

A map of the early 1800s shows that Armenian Street was once called Malay Lane, due to the Malay *kampong* settlement there. By 1808, the name had been changed to Armenian Lane. The Armenian trading community from India settled here, but instead of remaining in a neighbourhood between the Chulias and the Acehnese, sought social mobility by moving their houses to the suburbs and locating their church at Bishop Street.

The Armenians founded St. Gregory's Church in 1822, more than a decade before the Armenian Church in Singapore. In 1937, the church land was sold and the graves were transferred to a mass grave in the Western Road cemetery (see also Western Road).

A prominent Armenian clan was the family of Arratoon Anthony (after whom Arratoon Road is named). The Anthonys were among the Armenian diaspora that settled in Shiraz in Persia, and then in Bombay and Calcutta before coming to Penang.

But by far the most famous Armenians in the region were the Sarkies brothers who made their mark as hoteliers of the Eastern & Oriental in Penang and of the Raffles in Singapore (see also E & O Hotel, Farquhar Street). By the 1920s, most of the Penang Armenians had emigrated, largely to Singapore, and from there on to Hong

Several Eurasian Catholic families still reside at Argus Lane today.

Kong and Sydney where there are significant Armenian minorities.

A few houses on Armenian Street may have survived from the time when the Armenians lived here. These houses were probably retrofitted to function like shophouses when the Straits Chinese took over the neighbourhood.

A mid-19th century braziery run by Mohamed Tahir, where all sorts of brass and copper wares were sold, gave Armenian Street its Chinese Hokkien name, *Pak Thang-Ah Kay* (Coppersmith's Street).

In 1826, the death of Tengku Syed Hussain, founder of the Acheen Street Mosque, left a vacuum in the Acheen Street community leadership. Much of his family property was left to religious charity (waqf) or was bought over by Hokkien traders (see also Acheen Street).

The five great Hokkien clans *(Goh Tai Seng)* - namely, the Cheah, the

Khoo, the Yeoh, the Tan and the Lim - were led by prominent Straits Chinese. In the mid-19th century, they gradually established their clan houses in this area, with entrances along the trading street (see also Beach Street).

At the same time, the Hokkien-dominated secret society called *Khian Teik* set up its base at the Tua Pek Kong Temple in Armenian Street.

The Khian Teik allied itself with the Red Flag secret society (see also Acheen Street) - two chiefs of the latter were Syed Mohamed

Above, at left, the entrance to the Hokkien Tua Pek Kong Temple at No. 57 Armenian Street; next to it is a corner coffeeshop; at right, the Yap Temple. Below, the street's graceful curves.

Alatas and Che Long who lived in Armenian Street. The whole area, intensively built with institutional bases surrounded by members' houses, was turned into a Khian Teik-Red Flag stronghold.

During the Penang Riots of 1867, the Khian Teik-Red Flag alliance fought with the Ghee Hin-White Flag alliance for control of George Town (see also Rope Walk). Armenian Street was one of the scenes of fighting, where European volunteer police and their *sepoys* had to erect stockades. The entire town was laid siege for ten days, while reinforcements for both sides came from as far as Province Wellesley and Phuket.

Over the next few decades, smaller clashes continued to occur, until secret societies were finally suppressed in 1890. By that time, the Khian Teik had asserted their control, which allowed the Hokkien traders to emerge as the dominant force in Penang.

HOKKIEN TUA PEK KONG TEMPLE

Hock Teik Cheng Sin, popularly known as the Tua Pek Kong Temple, is dedicated to the God of Prosperity. The temple is accessible through a narrow gateway at 57 Armenian Street and a secret passage through one of the row of shophouses owned by the temple.

The carefully concealed temple was the former base of the Khian Teik secret society (also known as the *Tua Pek Kong Society)* founded by Khoo Teng Pang in the 1840s.

A low wall behind the Tua Pek Kong temple allowed members to cross

from the temple enclosure to the adjacent Khoo Kongsi (see also Cannon Square).

When secret societies were outlawed in 1890, the Khian Teik reconstituted itself and transferred its assets to several registered societies, namely the *Poh Hock Seah, Hokkien Kongsi, Cheng Hoe Seah* and *Tong Kheng Seah,* all of which are still based in this temple today.

The Poh Hock Seah carries on the religious traditions of the Khian Teik (see also Tua Pek Kong Temple, Tanjung Tokong).

The secret society prohibition resulted in the formation of many new Chinese associations in the early 1890s. The wealth of former secret societies was channelled into the great reconstruction of association buildings and temples at the turn of the century.

YAP KONGSI

The Yap Kongsi is located on land donated by Yeap Chor Ee, founder of the Ban Hin Lee Bank. The Straits Eclectic building dated 1924 was designed by Chew Eng Eam, and the adjoining temple which is dedicated to the patron deities was built in the 1950s. The temple was refurbished in the 1990s,

Winter solstice celebrations at the Cheah Kongsi.

with the addition of a decorated porch roof and dragon columns as well as a polygonal incendiary for joss paper.

CHEAH KONGSI

The Cheahs who originate from Sek Tong village in South China are members of the Cheah association founded in 1820 by Penang's pioneer settler Cheah Yam (see also Che Em Lane).

Upon his death, his widow Ong Sin Neoh took charge. She created a trust body and laid down the rules, thus becoming the only woman ever to wield such direct influence over a local Hokkien clan association. Cheah Yam's son Cheah Choo Yew, his grandsons and great-grandson have served as Presidents of the Cheah Kongsi.

The Cheah Kongsi was the first of the five great Hokkien clans to be established in Penang, with an endowment that includes a large group of early 19th century rentable properties.

The Cheah Kongsi has a charming front lawn and serene inner courtyards. The mid-19th century temple building uniquely integrates the double-storey porched bungalow plan with a Chinese courtyard plan. The worship hall proper is located on the upper floor. The temple porch was renovated in the 1930s with the addition of British lionheads. The roof decorations feature sirens, dogs, lions of stucco and shards of both Chinese and Dutch crockery. Just as eclectic are the old office building and its interior which combine Malay, Chinese and European elements.

Above left, the Cheah Kongsi temple - lionheads add to the charm. Above right, roof detail shows a siren at the gable. Below, the Straits Eclectic-style office building.

DR. SUN YAT SEN'S PENANG BASE

This late 19th century shophouse at 120 Armenian Street was the base of the Southeast Asia Tung Meng Hooi when it was headquartered in Penang from 1909 to 1911.

The Tung Meng Hooi was the party of Dr. Sun Yat Sen alias Sun Chong San, leader of the Chinese nationalist revolution. From Penang, Dr. Sun and his friends planned the Canton Uprising of Spring 1911. The historic "Penang Conference" took place in November 1910 at the Tung Meng Hooi headquarters.

Although the Canton Uprising was defeated, it was considered the turning point of the revolution which led to the Double Tenth Revolution, the overthrow of the Ching dynasty and the establishment of the first Republic in Asia.

A grand memorial was built at Hwang Hwa Kang to 72 fallen heroes of the Canton Uprising. Of the known martyrs, 24 were Nanyang Chinese, of whom the most posthumously famous was Malaya's Luo Ching Huo.

Dr. Sun Yat Sen, the first provisional President of the Republic, is generally considered the father of modern China.

Dr. Sun Yat Sen's Penang Base was the focal point of the progressive Chinese of that period. In their efforts to promote a greater social awareness among the Nanyang Chinese, Dr. Sun and his Penang friends and supporters made lasting contributions to the local society (see also Goh Say Eng's Business Premises, Armenian Street, and Philomatic Union, Macalister Road).

The Kwong Wah Jit Poh which was founded in Rangoon was then revived in this house as a daily paper in 1910. It is regarded as one of the longest running Chinese newspapers today.

The Malay-speaking community in the Acheen Street area was also aware of the anti-Manchu revolutionaries who were operating in the neighbourhood around the same time. The group was referred to as *orang Sun Yat Sen yang potong thauchang,* that is, the followers of Dr. Sun Yat Sen who cut off their pigtails in protest against Manchu rule in China (see also Acheen Street).

The "dwelling house or messuage" was already extant in 1875. At the time, the owner was Cheah Joo Seang, a trustee of the Cheah Kongsi from 1879 to 1895.

From 1900 to 1913, the shophouse belonged to Lim Boon Yeow. In the 1926, the house was taken over by a gun dealer Ch'ng Teong Swee, the author's maternal grandfather, and until recently it was used as a godown for his company *Ch'ng Eng Joo.*

The shophouse in the middle was the venue of the 1910 Penang Conference.

SYED ALATAS MANSION

Syed Mohamed Alatas (or Al-Attas) succeeded Che Long as the leader of the Red Flag secret society. During the Dutch siege on Aceh in the late 19th century, Syed Mohamed Alatas ran an arms smuggling trade. He obtained guns, cannons and ammunition from British India and supplied them to the Sultan of Aceh and the anti-Dutch resistance.

After his death in the 1890s, his son Syed Sheikh Alatas inherited the leadership of the Red Flag and carried it into the early 20th century.

Syed Alatas' first wife was reputedly a Malay of royal descent. He also married a daughter of the Chinese pepper trader and secret society leader, Khoo Tiang Poh (see also Carnarvon Street).

Syed Alatas' mid-19th century mansion at 128 Armenian Street is a well-preserved example of an early Straits Eclectic-style Muslim bungalow.

The mansion belongs to the Municipal Council and was restored in a pilot restoration project conducted with French technical assistance and sponsored by the Federal, State and Municipal governments. The Penang state government started the Heritage Centre, Penang, in these premises in 1996. The restoration was recognized with a best project award by the Badan Warisan Malaysia (Malaysian National Trust) in 1999.

Above, the Arab mansion on Armenian Street. In more recent times, the building has been used by Indians dealing in second-hand materials. Below, the well-ventilated historic interior.

AYER ITAM ROAD

A famous painting by Robert Smith depicts "The Chinese Mills" of Ayer Itam. The Hakka miller Low Amee supplied flour and bread to the whole town as well as to visiting ships. He also ran a tavern, which Captain Welsh, who married Light's daughter Sarah, visited in 1818. There, they were treated to a simple meal of plain rice and salted fish.

Welsh described Amee's establishment as "a capital house, but devoid of furniture, the poor industrious owner having been largely ruined by the non-payment of numerous quondam (former) guests who ate and drank in his hotel, but forgot to leave any equivalent in return".

Amee's men entertained the guests by performing antics with chopsticks, apparently a specialised kungfu art.

The Chinese Mills stood at the site of the present Lower Hill Railway Station, and the original brick work and granite can still be seen scattered around the river bed.

Though densely populated today, Ayer Itam maintains its rustic charm as a market town which sells produce from the surrounding hill farms. The country air is fresher than in George Town, as are the ingredients cooked by several open-air restaurants here.

The Ayer Itam valley has some of the richest soil on the island, yielded by the *Sungai Ayer Itam* (Black Water River) and its northern tributary *Sungai Ayer Putih* (White Water River). The area was cleared by Chinese settlers during Light's time.

Pepper, the island's first major crop, was introduced from Aceh in 1790 by Koh Lay Huan (see also China Street), and first cultivated in the Ayer Itam valley. This enterprise was sponsored by Francis Light in a programme to establish the island's agricultural base.

The Chinese Mills, Captain Robert Smith, 1818

Not far from Light's own Suffolk estate was the East India Company's 130-acre spice plantations in the valley itself. In 1822, the first Government Botanic Gardens were started in the vicinity. It supplied seed for the Company's plantations and vegetables for the officers' tables until 1834.

Today, cultivation has spread to the hills. Trails criss-cross the vegetable farms and fruit orchards, wind around the Ayer Itam Dam at 700 feet above sea level and ultimately link Ayer Itam to the Penang Botanic Gardens, Balik Pulau and Telok Bahang.

Since olden days, the Chinese have regarded the Ayer Itam hills as a geomantically important site. Known as *He San* (Crane Hill), these hills are recommended as a retreat for serious Taoist practitioners striving to attain immortality.

The east-facing slopes which overlook the sea are dotted with hill temples with granite stairs leading to them. The largest and best known of these is the Kek Lok Si, said to be positioned in the eye of the crane.

Like the ownership segregation between Europeans and Asians once observed on Penang Hill, a pecking order prevails in the supernatural society. Major deities reside on the hill slopes while the foothills are the abode of numerous *Datok Kong* - local spirits honoured by the Chinese - such as the *Tujuh Beradik* (Seven Brothers) and *Tok Bidan* (Grandfather Midwife).

Reflecting such animist beliefs are two interesting road names, *Jalan Batu Jantan* and *Jalan Batu Perempuan,* literally, "Male Rock Road" and "Female Rock Road". The two large rocks are believed to have rolled over and mated, once upon a time.

KEK LOK SI

The "Pure Land Temple", sometimes called "Temple of Supreme Bliss" is the country's largest temple complex, staggered on a 10-acre hill site. It harbours a well-equipped monastery for Buddhist monks and nuns. Judging from the number of souvenir shops, it is also one of Penang's most established tourist attractions.

The Kek Lok Si project was mooted by Beow Lean, then the chief monk of the Goddess of Mercy Temple at Pitt Street. The Kek Lok Si was established as a branch of the Buddhist Vatican in Drum Mountain in Foochow, Hokkien province. Beow Lean became its first abbot.

The Five Great Sponsors were the leading Hakka tycoons Cheong Fatt Tze, his cousin

The garden of calligraphed rocks and the pagoda of ten thousand Buddhas.

Chang Yu Nan, Cheah Choon Seng, Tye Kee Yoon and Chung Keng Kooi (see also Leith Street). With the support of the consular representatives of China in Penang, the project gained the imperial sanction of the Manchu Emperor Kuang Hsi, with a tablet and a gift of 70,000 volumes of the Imperial Edition of the Buddhist Sutras.

Construction began in 1893 and was completed in 1905. Even in those days, fund-raisers were experienced enough to dedicate structures and artefacts to the temple's benefactors.

During festival days, the complex is strung with thousands of lanterns representing donations by devotees. Long marches by hundreds of monks from Thailand are staged once or twice a year.

The *Pagoda of Rama VI* the foundation stone of which was laid by the Thai monarch, was completed in 1930. It combines a Chinese octagonal base, middle tiers of Thai architecture and a Burmese crown, reflecting the temple's wide embrace of Mahayana and Theravada Buddhism.

The "Pagoda of Ten Thousand Buddhas", as it is popularly called, is one of the few things left untouched by the drastic redevelopments in recent years.

PENANG HILL STATION

Many of the hill bungalows were constructed just after the completion of the Penang Hill Railway in the 1920s. The railway played a major role in democratising Penang Hill, which was until then an exclusive hill station of the European elite.

The funicular railway, designed by A.R. Johnson of the F.M.S Railway in 1922, was then considered an engineering feat in this part of the world. The subordinate engineers were Ceylonese and Indians, while the labour force mainly comprised Tamil Hindu road

builders. The dangerous construction work claimed several lives.

JADE EMPEROR'S PAVILION

Thnee Kong Thnua attracts a throng of worshippers during the celebrations on the eve of the Jade Emperor's birthday, which falls on the eighth night of the Chinese New Year.

The temple, located on a hill slope next to the hill railway track, features an interesting split-level layout. It has the only multi-bracketed dome of its kind in the country.

MAUSOLEUM OF SHEIKH OMAR BASHEER

Sheikh Omar Basheer Al-Khalidi from Hadhramaut was a religious teacher, reformist and imam of Acheen Street Mosque (see also Acheen Street). He was a Naqshabandiah Sufi who practised a special form of meditation called *suluk* in Kampong Melayu.

The outstanding multi-bracketed dome of the Jade Emperor's Pavilion

Sheikh Omar settled in this village at the invitation of his disciple Syed Hassan Al-Haru, the founder of the original Air Itam Mosque. Syed Hassan had inherited the land from his adopted father, Bacon, a writer in the service of Francis Light.

Sheikh Omar died in 1881 and was buried beside his house in Kampong Melayu. His son, Sheikh Zachariah, had the mausoleum constructed by builders from India and after his death in 1926 was himself buried in the mausoleum. Zachariah's son Dato' Haji Fathil Basheer, lived here until his death in 1994.

ANTI-WAR MEMORIAL

Of those who died in Penang during the Japanese Occupation, over 700 are buried here. The memorial also contains a special dedication to the martyrs among the Chinese machinery workers of Penang who joined the Anti-Japanese resistance movement in China in the 1930s and 1940s.

RAMA TEMPLE

The oldest Hindu Temple on the island was founded by Ranee Dhoby, the "Queen of Launderers", who provided laundry service for the East India Company officers and their families.

The site was granted in 1802. The original Ranee Dhoby Kuil forms the inner sanctum of the enlarged Rama Temple, which also encloses Ranee's tomb.

The historic Indian community of launderers is still washing clothes at Dhoby Ghaut just downstream from Suffolk House, at the confluence where the Ayer Itam and Waterfall Rivers flow into the Pinang River. *Ghaut* is an Indian word for steps leading to the water.

The entrance to the temple is from York Road, through the Dhoby Ghaut village, which the Tamils call *Vannan Thora Tedal*.

Left, the Anti-War Memorial near the Ayer Itam roundabout. Right, the domed resting place of Sheikh Omar Basheer in Kampung Melayu.

SUFFOLK HOUSE

"I give and bequeath likewise unto the aforesaid Martina Rozells, the pepper Gardens with my Garden house plantations and all the Land by me cleared in that part of this Island called Suffolk ...".

Thus wrote Light in his will in 1794. Suffolk Estate, named after his county of birth, was Light's legacy to his common-law wife Martina. Light was known to have built a colonnaded mansion on his estate - this would be *Suffolk House,* an Anglo-Indian Garden House which was a Georgian-style masonry bungalow surrounded by a garden.

After Light's death, the house was revived more than ten years later by W. E. Phillips, who was usually given the credit for building it. Suffolk House served as the Governor's Residence for Phillips and his father-in-law J. A. Bannerman, both who repeatedly served as Acting Governors of Penang at various times.

During Phillips' time the residence was enjoyed by his charmed circle, the Penang elite, and praised by visitors from far and wide. According to the watercolourist James

Above, Suffolk House, waiting to be restored. Below, Suffolk House as painted by Captain Robert Smith in 1818.

Wathen, there was "a very splendid mansion built in a mixed style of English and Indian architecture" in 1811.

In 1818, Suffolk House was lauded by Captain Welsh as

"one of the prettiest spots I have ever beheld. In the midst of a fine extensive lawn, surrounded by majestic trees and a box hedge, with a clean brook meandering through the centre, stands the noble and commodious house, with a park and aviary in its front, and the hill gradually receding in the background, crowned with wood of the richest foliage.... Italy itself could not produce a more verdant or lovely landscape."

In the same year, Raffles dined in the *Marble Hall,* with its chequered marble floor, as a guest of Governor Bannerman. Crawfurd reported the party's discussions about establishing a British port east of Malacca, which later turned out to be Singapore.

In its prime, Suffolk House was featured by Captain Robert Smith and other 19th century painters. After many changes in ownership, Suffolk House was used as the canteen of the Methodist Boys' School, until it was abandoned more than a decade ago.

Today, Suffolk House stands as a grand ruin. It is almost completely hidden from Ayer Itam Road by the school building, but is still surrounded by green open space on the bank of the Ayer Itam River.

The restoration of old Suffolk House has been proposed as part of a public project, that would include the creation of a linear heritage park along the river banks. The project is spearheaded by the Penang Heritage Trust and is now supported by the Public Works Department. Once used for all the major receptions and weddings on the island, Suffolk House restored to its former glory could serve as a distinguished social venue and Penang's premier cultural tourism attraction.

AYER RAJAH ROAD

Teluk Ayer Rajah is the bay between George Town and Tanjung Tokong. By 1796, over two thousand acres of the area had been cleared by Europeans, Eurasians, Malays, Chinese, Siamese, Burmese and Indians.

Today, Ayer Rajah Road is lined with teak trees, and flanked by plush suburban houses. It is also the address of the Thai Consulate, the Indonesian Consultate and the quarters of senior government officers.

TUNKU ABDUL RAHMAN'S RESIDENCE

Tunku Abdul Rahman (1903-1990) became the first Prime Minister of Malaysia in 1957. The prince of Kedah who negotiated the country's independence is remembered as the country's father, *Bapa Malaysia.*

When the Tunku was preparing for retirement, he accidentally ran into a good friend, who told him about two houses on offer. He saw No. 14 and No. 16 Ayer Rajah Road and took a liking to the second one, built in 1929. Reflecting on the circumstances that affected his decision, he named his home *Takdir,* which means "fate".

The Tunku chose to spend his last years in Penang, and the road on which he lived was renamed after him.

The Tunku spent his last years in Takdir, the house that fate chose.

BANGKOK LANE

The street next to the Siamese temple is flanked by two rows comprising forty link houses built in 1928 by Cheah Leong Kah, who started out making and repairing horse carriages and then pioneered motor firms in Penang.

The architect was Chew Eng Eam, one of the early western-trained Chinese architects, who also designed the Khoo Sian Ewe complex (see Loke Thye Kee, Burmah Road).

BATU GANTONG ROAD

Batu Gantong, which means "Hanging Rock", is the site of the Hokkien cemeteries.

It was also the pen-name of Chan Kim Boon, a translator of Chinese classics into Baba Malay. This is an unusual instance of a person named after a place

Kim Boon's large body of works, including *The Three Kingdoms* in thirty volumes, was published in Singapore from 1890s to 1910s. They achieved great popularity among Straits Chinese readers.

Born in Penang, Kim Boon lived and worked in Teluk Ayer Street, Singapore, and maintained a second residence in his home town. When his Singapore friends came to Penang, they looked him up at Batu Gantong, only to find a vast cemetery. Kim Boon actually lived at 75 Muntri Street.

Accused of misleading them, the writer pointed out that Batu Gantong was his "permanent address", that is, the graveyard where he would eventually be buried.

The main attraction at Batu Gantong today, however, is not Chan Kim Boon's burial turf but the Penang Turf Club.

The architecturally successful ensemble at Bangkok Lane, by Chew Eng Eam.

PENANG TURF CLUB

Horse-racing was an established institution in the Straits Settlements. The Penang Turf Club was founded in 1864 and formerly had a Race Course along Macalister Road. The club acquired this 230-acre site in 1935. Among the assets removed to the new grounds was a pretty cast iron fountain donated in 1904 by Chung Thye Pin, an avid racer.

At the turn of the century, both jockeys and griffins were largely imported from Australia. Race horses were imported from Victoria, broken in and trained at the Pinang Horse Repository, before being sold to private owners.

Today, a small community of Baweans (locally called 'Boyans'), from an island north of Java, live next to the race course. The young boys are employed as syces.

A romantic gift from a horse-lover.

BEACH STREET

Northern Beach Street is the financial centre of George Town, with a rich collection of highly individualistic commercial buildings designed by famous architects in the latest styles of their time.

Penang's historic trading street used to run along the waterfront during Francis Light's time. European traders were concentrated in the north near the important piers and government offices.

The street was lined with trading stores, hence the Malays remember it as *Jalan Gedung* (Street of Godowns).

The road was gradually widened as the early buildings were replaced in the late 19th century with large and prestigious commercial developments which had offices for rent on the upper floors and retail lots on the ground floor.

The European exclusivity of northern Beach Street was broken by enterprises like Goon Yen & Friends and Goh Taik Chee & Co. which were owned by Chinese *towkays* but managed along European lines.

Many improvements in amenities were first tried out on Beach Street. In the 1870s petroleum lamps were installed on a trial basis by Huttenbach (see also Huttenbach's Godowns, Jelutong). This privately-conducted demonstration of street lighting and its benefits convinced the Municipal Commisioners, and Huttenbach was awarded the contract to light up the streets of George Town for the next four decades.

In 1894, a short section of Beach Street, between Union and Bishop Streets, was the first to be tarred. The experiment proved

rather expensive, and serious tarring only began ten years later, after the first car was introduced in 1903. The problem of dust then became urgent, for untarred thoroughfares had to be hosed down several times a day.

The second half of Beach Street, dominated by Chinese wholesalers, extended further south as trading activities grew. The wholesalers' shops are unusually long, with high ceilings and ample warehouse space at the back. Large hooks hanging from the beam over the five-foot way are used for weighing goods.

Today, trade is done with traditional scales, abacus and telephone. The idle appearance of these shopfronts most of the day belies the large volumes of trade actually carried out behind the scenes.

According to its Chinese names, Beach Street is divided into a number of sections, reflecting the varying identities from north to south.

The northernmost end was referred to as *Ang Mo Tho Koh Kay* (European Commercial Street). Between Chulia and Armenian Streets was the section called *Tiong Kay* (Central Street) of the Chinese wholesalers.

Above, Logan's Buildings, once the leading commercial complex. Below, the general store Whiteway, Laidlaw & Co. opened here in this block in 1903.

44

KONGSOON HOUSE

Erected in 1914, Kongsoon House was the premises of Goh Teik Chee & Co, wholesale store and ship chandlers, suppliers of mining, engineering and industrial machinery.

Goh Teik Chee led the Anti-Opium movement, and was the first Chinese in Penang to be awarded the Order of the British Empire for helping to relieve the food shortage during the First World War.

Southwards towards Acheen Street was *Tuan Lo-Sin Kay* (Master Hussain's Street). Around this section are narrow gateways leading to the Hokkien traders' clan temples (see also Armenian Street).

Lower down were shops specialising in metalwork, hence *Pak Theek Kay* (Ironsmith's Street). Around Prangin Lane and Fish Lane is *Kiam Hu Thnia* (Salted Fish Yard).

Finally, the end of Beach Street is called *Sia Boey* (Town's End), as the Prangin River defined the boundary of the early town. The Malay name for the same section is *Hujung Pasir* (Sand's End).

LOGAN'S BUILDINGS

This late 19th century commercial block originally had European offices on the upper floors and retail stores on the ground floor. A granite-paved walkway leads to the mews in the back courtyard, formerly a convenient venue for public auctions.

The three-storey block was reduced to two storeys in the 1930s. The cast iron balconies and grillwork have been removed.

1886 BUILDING

Formerly Goon Yen & Friends, Chinese-owned general and retail stores run along western lines. The ground floor emporium featured an international range of goods and stylish displays which impressed even the well-travelled European consumer. The rest of the building was let out to offices such as Howarth Erskine Engineers.

Built in 1886, this is probably the oldest commercial building on Beach Street which survives in its original form.

Above, the corner Kongsoon House and the original OCBC Bank building designed by Charles Boutcher in 1938, next to it. Below, the 1886 Building, which can also be seen in the picture above, at far right.

Ban Hin Lee Bank

The Ban Hin Lee Bank was founded in Penang by Yeap Chor Ee in 1935.

Chor Ee built up his financial empire through wise investments, consolidating it during the slump of the early 1930s which saw the crash of many rubber fortunes (see also Homestead, Northam Road).

Although grown to a stature comparable to the nation-wide banks, Ban Hin Lee Bank remains "the one and only Penang-based bank". The handsome bank building was designed by Ung Ban Hoe of Stark & MacNeill in 1936.

ABN-AMRO Bank

The *Nederlandsche Handel Maatschappij* was founded in 1824 to promote Dutch trade, shipping and plantation interests abroad. Its functions were to "advise like a chamber of commerce, finance like a bank, and trade like a merchant". The Dutch bank was originally established in Penang in 1888 as the bank of the Netherlands Trading Society. The present building, designed by the architectural firm of Wilson & Neubronner, opened in 1905. It was restored for the bank's centenary by a Dutch architect from the Head Bank.

Around 1949, the Dutch Office in Penang moved from the Malayan Railway Building

to the Dutch Bank, and here it became the Indonesian Consultate.

The Standard Chartered Bank

The Penang Branch of the Chartered Bank of India, China and Australia was established in 1875, making it the oldest bank branch in the country. The present building, designed by the architectural firm of Stark & McNeill, was completed around 1930. It was renovated in 1992 and reopened with a new banking hall.

In the colonial era, the two foremost British exchange banks in the country were the Chartered Bank and the Hongkong & Shanghai Banking Corporation, who vied with each other to build the best bank building on Beach Street.

The British banks gave out loans through *chettiars* and Chinese compradors, and issued their own bank notes before the Straits currency was introduced.

Left, the Ban Hin Lee Bank. Above right, the Standard Chartered Bank building. Below right, the ABN-AMRO building, recently restored and converted into a café.

INDIA HOUSE

This commercial building was built in 1937 by S.N.A.S. Sockalingam Chettiar, said to have been the highest assessment payer of his time. Most people still remember the India House as the former premises of the United States Information Service (USIS).

GEDUNG ACEH OR ATJEH

The old *Acehnese Store* was originally a jail building already extant in 1805 - hence the thick walls and small windows on the ground floor. In the early 19th century, Tengku Syed Hussain acquired it for his office and spice godown, and subsequently added a shopfront (see also Acheen Street) and possibly additional floors. The result is a small towering structure reminiscent of the tall Arab buildings in Hadhramaut.

This prominent building was a landmark along the waterfront for boats that approached Acheen Street Ghaut. It was the first four-storey building in town and the Malays called it *Rumah Tinggi* (The Tall House). The Chinese named the junction of Acheen and Beach streets *Kuan Lau Ah* (Small Tower Junction); the ancient landmark stands at the end of the section of Beach Street which they still remember as "Master Hussain's Street".

BADJENID & SONS

A trader who started out in Acheen Street was Sheikh Mohamed Badjenid from Hadhramaut, South Yemen. In 1917, he opened a business to import spices from India, cloth from Indonesia and velvet from Persia.

Today, the Badjenid shops in Beach Street supply canvas, canopies and tarpaulins for lorries and *tongkang* boats. One section stocks a wide range of European and Indian perfumes such as *gulab, hina* and *hajar aswat*, and the *kain pelekat* or Indian sarong.

Above, the distinctive India House. Below, the Acehnese Godown, an ancient landmark.

KOE GUAN OFFICE

Khaw Soo Cheang was the patriarch of the famous Khaw family of Penang and South Thailand. He came as a penniless immigrant in the 1810s to Penang, where he started out as a vegetable farmer in Sungai Tiram. Several years later, he moved to South Thailand and opened a trading shop which he called *Koe Guan* (High Source).

Before the development of tin mining in Perak and Selangor, South Thailand was the most important tin-mining hinterland for Penang, generating much wealth for Penang's oldest families.

Soo Cheang rose to become Governor of Ranong in 1854. His sons later became Governors of Ranong, Kraburi, Langsuan, Trang and Kra, and their descendants are titled *Na Ranong*.

The most renowned administrator among them was Khaw Sim Bee, Superintendent Commissioner of Monkthon Phuket, who was assassinated in 1913. Shot by a gunman in Trang, he was brought to the General Hospital in Penang, but could not be saved.

The Khaw family built up an empire which included plantations and tin mines in South Thailand as well as international trading and tin smelting in Penang. With a group of close associates, they controlled Eastern Shipping and Eastern Smelting (see also Datuk Keramat Smelting).

Soo Cheang, who died in 1882, donated a playing field called *Ranong Ground* to the people of Penang. It is now the site of Dewan Sri Pinang. The Koe Guan Company office, set up in 63 Beach Street in the 1870s, continues to administer the Khaw Soo Cheang Trust.

Formerly a three-storey building which Soo Cheang used as an office and residence, it has been renovated to two storeys and now houses a small private exhibition on the Khaw family history in the first floor hall.

Behind this building is an early 19th century godown which originally stood on the waterfront, before the Weld Quay reclamation and the creation of Victoria Street.

The Khaw family's fleet of ships ran between Penang and Burma along the west coast of the Kra Ithmus, and engaged in coolie traffic. Their waterfront godowns accommodated new immigrants who had just got off the boat from China and were awaiting the next ship to take them to the tin mines of South Thailand.

The dilapidated building holds the memory of men who left behind their families in China and sailed to the Straits Settlements as *coolies* - which literally means, "hardship labour". The indentured labourers came prepared for the first few years of backbreaking work in the tin mines; beyond that, if they survived, lay the opportunity of making their fortunes in the Nanyang.

Coolies were accommodated in this early 19th century godown, next to the Victoria Street bus station.

BISHOP STREET

Bishop Garnault of Siam and his congregation escaped religious persecution in Ligor and Phuket in 1781. They fled to Kuala Kedah where they joined another 80 Catholics of Portuguese descent; some from Siam and others who had fled Malacca after the Dutch takeover.

The French priest met Light in Kuala Kedah and asked to relocate the Catholic Mission to Penang. Immediately after taking possession of the island, Light sent his ship *Speedwell* to fetch the Eurasians from Kedah.

The first Catholic Church was built on Church Street, and the Presbytery of Bishop Garnault on the adjacent Bishop Street.

When the priest left in 1787, Francis Light wrote to Bengal for a replacement, "A Portuguese padre would be better than a French, the latter being too great politicians."

The Armenian Church was founded here in 1822 (see also Armenian Street).

Around 1905, the Mercantile Bank of India moved into 1 Bishop Street (now De Silva's). The street later became known for the two premier department stores of their day - Whiteways (now Palmco Building) which moved there in 1914 and its close competitor, Pritchards. Several shops here sell Indian silks, which used to be a popular buy among European tourists.

As the centre of the early service industry, Bishop Street is lined with old-fashioned shops which used to cater to the European clientele - a piano shop, opticians, an old Nyonya restaurant, tailors for gentlemen as well as English-literate book stores, stationers and printing presses.

Their outdated facades are matched only by an equally vintage notion of service and pride in their trades.

Above, Rio Cafe, a corner coffeeshop that catches the breeze from the Esplanade, below, a gentleman's tailor.

Since the late 19th century, the section between Beach Street and Penang Street has been called *Chat Bok Ke* (Painting Wood Street) or *Cha Kang Ke* (Woodworking Street). The furniture shops here were the source of much of Penang's so-called colonial furniture - made by Cantonese craftsmen, often copied from European catalogues and customized to the client's requirements.

SAN WOOI WOOI KOON

An association of the Cantonese dialect group from San Wooi district, established in the 1870s. A side lane leads to a row of houses tucked away behind the temple.

BRICK KILN ROAD

The road cuts through an area known as *Bakar Bata*. The present city incinerator is suspected to be the former site of the 19th century brick kiln.

THE DIAMOND JUBILEE SIKH TEMPLE

The Sikhs first came to the country in 1881, recruited as paramilitary officers by Captain Speedy for the Perak Menteri during the tin wars. They later formed the majority of the Malay States Guides, a British regiment based in Taiping at the turn of the century.

In response to the Sikh community's request for land in Penang to build a *gurdwara* (Sikh temple), the Straits Settlements Government granted the site of the former police barracks at Brick Kiln Road in 1897, the year of Queen Victoria's Diamond Jubilee.

The Diamond Jubilee Sikh Temple, when completed in 1899, was the largest *gurdwara* in Southeast Asia. A month's salary was donated by each Sikh member of the Malay States Guides towards its construction.

The Sikh New Year and the Birthday of the Guru Nanak are celebrated here.

The sturdy Sikh men easily find employment as security officers - many retired soldiers and policemen became caretakers and watchmen.

Above, commercial architecture from the 1920s, originally United Engineers' building, now Public Bank building. Below, the Cantonese association guarded by a granite fence and a pair of lions (repainted).

BRIDGE STREET

Bridge Street runs along the sea from Anson Bridge, across the Prangin canal, to the bridge over the Pinang River.

This was the working-class quarter of the Hokkien community who supported the Khian Teik society. The 19th century triad controlled the route to the spice plantations in Glugor and to the Hokkien burial grounds in Batu Gantong and Batu Lanchang.

In 1879, its leader Khoo Thean Teik was one of the main benefactors of the *Seng Ong Beow,* which guards an important geomantic point (see also Cannon Street).

The shophouses along the whole length of Bridge Street are strikingly regular - most were rebuilt in the late 19th century, replacing houses of wood and attap which had been repeatedly set on fire by the rival society.

The street has been renamed Jalan C.Y. Choy after a Penang Socialist Front candidate

Above, a sturdy Sikh. Below, warehouses along Bridge Street. The woman in blue is one of a vanishing breed of female construction labourers from Hui Aun district, Hokkien province.

who became City Councillor and then Mayor of George Town from 1964-66.

C.Y. Choy was known for his extremely populist style - he would station himself in a five-foot way along this street, equipped with a typewriter, chair and desk to write petitions for his constituents.

THE TEMPLE OF THE CITY PROTECTOR

The *Seng Ong Beow* is dedicated to the City Protector-cum-Chief Magistrate of Hades, who presides over cases of injustice and corruption in the underworld. His portfolio makes him the patron deity of government officers and the police - the latter pay homage annually on the 15th day of the Chinese New Year.

The traditional Chinese oath-taking ritual requires one to behead a white cockerel before the deity. Such an oath is taken, for example, when one wishes either to swear loyalty to a gang or deny being a member, to adopt a child or to deny paternity.

Fortunately, the officials of Hades who bring you before the Chief Magistrate are known to accept opium as a bribe. For a small donation, the temple attendant will smear opium on the hanging tongues of *Tua Pek* and *Jee Pek* (Grand-Uncle and Second Uncle) on your behalf.

Detail of the Seng Ong Beow roof ridge.

BURMAH LANE

A Burmese community of fishermen and farmers settled in Pulau Tikus during Light's time. The Burmese village was known as *Kampong Ava*. Some educated Burmese were also brought in as government surveyors.

The Thai community settled here not long after the Burmese - the two communities observe Theravada Buddhism and have long since intermarried with the local Chinese.

The Burmese and Thai temples located on either side of Burmah Lane both attract large numbers of Chinese Buddhists. They are also established tourist draws.

Burmah Lane north of Kelawai Road was the original Brick Kiln Road, being the site of the Company's kilns in the early 1800s.

DHAMMIKARAMA BURMESE BUDDHIST TEMPLE

The first Buddhist temple on Penang island is the Burmese Temple founded in 1803, on land donated by Nyonya Betong. As financial patrons and dedicated volunteers, women devotees have been the mainstay of this and many other temples in Penang.

The oldest part is the stupa consecrated in 1805, enshrined within the outer stupa which was contructed in 1838 together with the adjacent ceremonial Sima Hall.

Much of the rest of the temple has been rebuilt in the last two decades. Now it features many colourful shrines and statues, the most fantastic of which is a pair of *Panca Rupa* "Guardian Protectors of the World". The beasts have elephant trunks, horse ears and hoofed legs, lion faces, deer horns, fish bodies and *garuda* wings, thus mastering the three realms of water, land and air.

with Siam, the land was generously granted by Queen Victoria in 1845. Governor Butterworth officially presented this grant to four women trustees.

The first monk was *Phorthan Kuat.* The "Powerful Monk", as he was called by the locals, loved to eat *laksa* - this food is still offered to his shrine today.

On *Thankyan,* Burmese New Year's day, folks young and old take licence to splash each other with water; those already doused stop running away and join the *rambong* dance.

WAT CHAIYA MANGKALARAM

The 33-metre Buddha, at last count the third longest in the world, is draped in a gold-leafed saffron robe and reclines on a large crematorium. As photography is not allowed inside the hall, this monument has to be seen with one's own eyes. The other popular attraction in this temple is the Wheel of Fortune which dispenses a paper fortune for a coin.

Behind the temple is a small Thai village as well as a Thai cemetery. The temple and Thai community already existed in the early 19th century.

As a gesture to promote trading relations

The Penang Thais maintain close ties with their relatives in South Thailand and the northern states of Malaysia. They have thus retained their language as well as cultural forms like the *Menora*, a ritual healing dance-theatre.

At this temple, the local Thais celebrate the traditional Buddhist festivals, the *Sonkran* which is the Thai New Year water festival, and the *Loy Krathong*, where candles are floated out to sea on small leaf-boats.

Above, the ancient Burmese stupa. Below, the dragons and yak which guard the Thai temple.

53

BURMAH ROAD

Burmah Road, which extends for about 3.7 kms, was an early road that cut through the plantations to the Burmese village (see also Burmah Lane). The Burmese village became part of Pulau Tikus, a town that has always been the home of Penang's Eurasian, Burmese and Thai minorities.

As the intermediate areas developed, the side roads were named after places in Burma which came under British influence - Rangoon, Mandalay, Tavoy, Irrawaddi, Salween and Moulmein.

At the town end of Burmah Road is a mosque called Mesjid Titik Papan (Plank Bridge Mosque) founded in 1893. It marks the point where the Prangin Canal, which used to come up as far as Transfer Road, used to be crossed by a drawbridge.

Several Chinese associations are lined up opposite the Art Deco-style Rex cinema. From the eastern end, the first is the Khek Asso-

ciation, partially demolished, whose facade now forms the gateway to a car park.

The second is *Khaw Si Koe Yang Tong*, the Khaw clan association to which our present Chief Minister Dr. Koh Tsu Koon belongs. Next to it is the Loh family temple, followed by the Goddess of Mercy Temple or *Kuan Yin See*, not to be confused with the one on Pitt Street.

The *Mesjid Tarek Ayer* at the junction of Aboo Siti Lane was founded in 1880. It marks the resting place for water-sellers who conveyed water from the Botanic Gardens to town by means of pails suspended on shoulder yokes.

Two important buildings on Burmah Road have been demolished in recent years.

The *Lin Radio* building, opposite the Lorong Selamat junction, was originally the residence of Mohd. Sheikh Ghani (see also York Road Mosque). The early 1900s building was the grandest and most ornate Muslim mansion in Penang.

Morningside, along Clove Hall Road, was

Government quarters from the 1920s are found along Burmah Road and the perpendicular streets like Madras Lane, Yahudi Road (now Jalan Zainal Abidin), Service Road, Irrawaddy Road and so forth.

a 19th century European residence which became the home of Cheah Kee Ee, an enlightened tin-miner who led the anti-polygamy movement. He was known to have furnished an excellent private library. His daughter married the illustrious Dr. Lim Chwee Leong at *Morningside* (see also Soo Beng Dispensary, Prangin Road).

The junction of Burmah Road and Cantonment Road is the heart of Pulau Tikus village, named after a small offshore island which looks like a mouse. Nearby is *Lorong Pulau Tikus* (Mouse Island Lane), which is next to *Lorong Kuching* (Cat Lane).

In the 1920s, Pulau Tikus became a choice resort suburb for the town elite to build their second homes. These country bungalows, typically raised like Malay houses, have been called "Sino-Malay-Palladian". Some also have Eurasian and Thai influences.

Today, Pulau Tikus is part of the George Town conurbation.

LOKE THYE KEE

This unique boat-shaped restaurant which dates from 1919 is the oldest extant Chinese restaurant in Penang. The pioneer cactuses are still thriving on the roof balconies.

It was started by two Hainanese brothers who were Khoo Sian Ewe's cooks. Their employer helped them realise their personal dream by releasing them from service and developing the restaurant premises.

Loke Thye Kee used to be a favourite match-making venue. Candidates of arranged marriages, properly accompanied by their families, would come here for discreet viewing. To confirm or decline the engagement, one or the other party would tactfully give a sign by taking tea in a certain way.

Nearby is the Majestic Theatre, which opened in 1926 as *The Penang Theatre,* and was also known alternatively as the *Khoo Sian Ewe Theatre.* It was the first cinema in Penang to screen Chinese talkies in the 1930s and Chinese locals called it the *Shanghai Sound Movie Theatre.*

Loke Thye Kee and Majestic Theatre are part of an ensemble of buildings along Khoo Sian Ewe Road, Phee Choon Road and Penang Road, which was designed in the 1920s by the architect Chew Eng Eam for Khoo Sian Ewe (see also Bangkok Lane and Wing Look, Penang Road).

Khoo Sian Ewe, the largest private landowner in the prewar decades, was the doyen of the Straits Chinese community of his time. He headed the Penang Chinese Chamber of Commerce, the Penang Chinese Town Hall, the Khoo Kongsi and numerous other institutions. Of his sons, the most distinguished in public service is Dato' Khoo Keat Siew.

The "love boat" restaurant, formerly a match-making venue.

KUAN YIN SEE

During the Nine Emperor Gods Festival the Kuan Yin See is the focus of a vegetarian food festival. Kuan Yin See is the *other* Goddess of Mercy Temple, not to be confused with the more famous one on Pitt Street.

The temple was adapted from a bungalow donated by a Kek Lok Si abbot in 1923. Bathroom tiles on the facade were a 1980s addition.

A famous resident monk was Fa Kong, whose name means "Empty Dharma". He was Penang's foremost advocate of *Chen* Buddhism (from which Japanese *Zen* derives).

Fa Kong's eccentricities included a love for acrobatics and animals - he entered his dogs for competitions in England, and built a zoo in Ayer Itam (hence "Zoo Road") from lottery winnings. A famous Zen verse composed by him is inscribed on a rock in the Kek Lok Si garden.

LOH LEONG SAN'S FAMILY RESIDENCE

The well-maintained ensemble of four houses has kept the original colour scheme that was widely used in the Chinese Straits Eclectic homes of the early 20th century.

The Chinese consider green a perennial colour and embraced certain Victorian colour schemes - hence, the walls are jade green, the windows louvres are apple green, the frames are of a darker green, the details are picked out in white and so forth.

However, the older and by far the most common colour used on George Town's historic buildings was indigo blue. If all the prewar houses in town were restored to their original colours, half of George Town would be a pale shade of indigo.

CHURCH OF IMMACULATE CONCEPTION

The Portuguese Eurasian community first settled at Pulau Tikus in the 18th century (see also Bishop Street and Ayer Rajah Road).

The green-on-green colour scheme of Loh Leong San's residence.

Though they faced religious persecution, a small Catholic community remained in Phuket until the Phya Tak Massacre of 1810.

Then the survivors, led by Father John Baptist Pasqual, came over to Penang. They settled in Pulau Tikus at the invitation of Pasqual's niece Thomasia Pasqual and several other families, namely the Jeremiahs, the Gregorys and the Josephs.

Pasqual built a church at Kelawai Road, next to the present Catholic cemetery, before the arrival of the French mission (see also Kelawai Road). The land between College Lane and Leandro's Lane, donated to the early Catholic refugees, is today known as *Kampong Serani* (Eurasian Village).

The Church of Immaculate Conception was established in the early 1800s, together with the historic Eurasian village. The present church building was constructed in 1899 and last renovated in the 1970s.

Having settled on the Malay peninsula since the 16th century, the Portuguese Eurasians are a unique local community. They adopted many elements of the Malay lifestyle - speaking Malay, wearing sarongs and living in *kampong* houses - while adhering to the Catholic religion.

Though few in numbers, the Penang Eurasians have made great social contributions especially in the fields of education and the arts (see also Jimmy Boyle's House, Kelawai Road).

Kampong Serani has been regarded by generations of settlers as *Tanah Wakaf,* that is, religious charity land held in trust by the Church for the Catholic Poor.

The village had an assortment of traditional timber houses, including an early Catholic school building known as *Noah's Ark*.

In spite of its great cultural significance, this historic home of the Eurasian community was largely demolished to make way for development in 1992.

Above, the Church of Immaculate Conception. Below, one of the few original houses remaining in Kampong Serani (Kampong Serani demolished).

CAMPBELL STREET

The Chinese call Campbell Street *Sin Kay* because it was a "new street" created between Pitt Street and Penang Road in the mid-19th century.

However, *Sin Kay* by way of pun came to refer to the "fresh prostitutes" brought in from China to fill the courtesans quarters along this street. The Malay name *Jalan Nona Baru,* or "street of new maidens", is just as explicit.

The traditional red light district flourished until the war. The houses of pleasure were identified by red lanterns hung at the door. Senior citizens recall these dens as places to relax and enjoy a range of services. The well-dressed, well-mannered courtesans served opium, tea and liqour, and provided musical entertainment and companionship.

Another Malay name for the street is *Jalan Makau.* The Cantonese were also called Macao people because Macao was the main port of emigration for the people from Kwangtung province. In the late 19th century, these included a great number of Cantonese coolies and prostitutes.

More recently, Campbell Street has become a retail shopping street where locals can still buy their watches, shoes, bags and textiles in shophouses rather than department stores. Here are also Chinese medicine halls and jewellery stores, popular dim-sum and chicken rice shops like *Thor Yuen,* and two well-known Indian Muslim restaurants *Hamidyaah* and *Taj.*

CAMPBELL STREET MARKET

The municipal market was built around 1900, on part of the former Kapitan Kling Mosque burial ground (see also Pitt Street).

The Malays referred to the market site as *Hutan Mayat* or "Forest of Corpses". The compensation received by the mosque was used to purchase the Perak Road cemetery

The only chickens on Campbell Street today are in the market.

lands. Thus the graves were removed - with one possible exception.

On the market grounds is a shrine known as *Keramat Mustafa Wali*, dedicated to the patron saint of poulterers - could this have been a tomb left behind from the "Forest of Corpses"?

The corner market building, with its ornate cast iron columns and brackets, is a smaller version of the late Victorian markets like Covent Garden in London or the Teluk Ayer Market in Singapore. Its original unrendered brick facade was painted over several years ago when a paint company sponsored the Municipal Council's efforts to spruce up its heritage buildings.

Happily, the Campbell Street Market has survived as a wet market - you can still watch chickens being slaughtered here. In the mornings, market activities spill out onto the northern section of Carnarvon Street, which is closed to traffic during peak hours.

CANNON SQUARE

A cannon shot fired during the secret society fights known as the Penang Riots of 1867 supposedly made a large hole in the ground in this area (see also Armenian Street).

Khoo Thean Teik, who was convicted for instigating the riots, was the Khian Teik secret society's most notorious "Elder Brother", and at the same time a director of the Leong San Tong Khoo Kongsi at Cannon Square (see also Boon San Tong, Victoria Street). Thean Teik was sentenced to death, but the colonial government feared that his execution would cause another outbreak.

The sentence was commuted to life imprisonment, and in the end he was released after only seven years.

The former criminal quickly established himself as a businessman and acquired respectability. He prospered, owning vast plantations near Ayer Itam town now known as Thean Teik Estate.

In his old age, Thean Teik donated heavily to temples and cemeteries. He finally became part of the establishment when he became a founder of the Penang Chinese Town Hall in 1881.

After 1890, the Hokkien clan associations succeeded in institutionalising themselves as the established Chinese families of Penang. Prominent Khoos retained leadership of the Penang Hokkien community until the war. Accordingly, the Khoo Kongsi spared no expense to build a permanent monument to its own legitimacy.

KHOO KONGSI

The famous Khoo Kongsi on Cannon Square is the grandest clan temple in the country. It is also the city's greatest historic attraction. The clan temple has retained its authentic historic setting, which includes an association building, a traditional theatre and late 19th century rowhouses for clan

Khoo Kongsi's rentable properties along Cannon Street - terrace houses developed in the late 1930s, after a fire consumed the original 19th century row.

members, all clustered around a granite-paved square.

The Khoo Kongsi is meant only for members of the *Leong San Tong* (Dragon Mountain Hall) clan, whose forefathers came from *Sin Kang* clan village in Hokkien province, where all are descended from a common progenitor.

Sin Kang is located in Chuan Chew state in the Hokkien province; the port is well known for its historic Muslim communities. In Penang, the Khoo clan became close allies of their Muslim neighbours through the common trade with Aceh.

The Khoos were among the wealthy Baba traders of 17th century Malacca. The pioneer Khoos were already well established in Penang when they formed the Leong San Tong Khoo Kongsi in 1835 and acquired the land in 1851.

The clan complex at Cannon Square is the best physical expression of the traditional social system which the Hokkien clans created in the Straits Settlements - a feudal system adapted to an urban context in a foreign land.

It was in fact a miniature clan village. The rowhouses, originally reserved for clan members, formed a veritable fortress at the centre of which was the clan temple, the offices and the square for social activities and festivals.

The complex was accessible through the formal entrance at Beach Street, a side entrance at Armenian Street and a carriageway (formerly with a wooden gate) at Cannon Street. Signs over these small gateways denote *Sin Kang,* the clan village.

The clan governed its own, with a board of directors responsible for the management, and a senate of elders who drew the rules and settled internal disputes. The association also had a strong welfare function - it provided schooling for the children, paid funeral expenses for those who died impecunious and took care of the widows and orphans.

In the 19th century, the Chinese clan associations were the kinship organisations through which the already established settlers helped their newly immigrant relatives make a place in the local society.

Above, the ornate formal entrance gate at Beach Street. Below, the 19th century office building.

The clan *kongsi* functioned as the clan incorporated - it loaned money for business ventures and invested in real estate. Today, the Khoo Kongsi is one of the richest social organisations in Penang, amply endowed with rentable properties.

The clan temple itself is a monument of *Zhang Zhou* architecture of typical late Ch'ng dynasty baroqueness. Built in 1906 by craftsmen from China, it replaced a temple building, reputedly even more magnificent, which had burnt down several years earlier. The fire was explained with the story that the grandeur of the original temple provoked the gods.

The clan temple is dedicated to the clan's patron deities and also houses a collection of ancestral tablets. Chinese opera is still staged at the theatre during the seventh lunar month. Permission to enter the clan temple can be obtained from the adjacent association building, open during office hours.

Above, the Khoo Kongsi at Cannon Square - the grandest clan temple in the country. Below, educating a group of students on Zhang Zhou architecture and the role of 19th century Chinese clan associations.

Chinese worship, assorted eathernware and crockery, art materials and Chinese books.

Pitt Street originally continued down to the Prangin Canal. Lower Pitt Street, already extant in the mid-19th century, was later renamed Carnarvon Street after the Earl of Carnarvon, Secretary of State for the Colonies in the 1870s.

CARNARVON STREET

This is the street of undertakers, coffin-makers and *kong-teik* craftsmen. The last refer to makers of funerary paper artefacts.

Elaborate paper houses, complete with paper Mercedez Benzes, servants, clothes, televisions, credit cards, videotapes of the deceased's favorite movies and generally anything that one can think of which the dead may need in the next world - all these are miniaturised in the form of paper offerings and dispatched to the spirits by way of burning.

Paper money and clothes are burnt several times a year, during certain festivals in honour of the dead, including the anniversary of death. The dead need a regular supply of new clothes and money - the latter to bribe guards and judges of the underworld.

Besides these morbid activities, Carnarvon Street also has shops selling accessories for

In the days of secret societies (see also Armenian Street and Rope Walk), the wide thoroughfare separated the largely Hokkien neighbourhood to the east, and the Cantonese-Teochew neighbourhood to the west.

The Chinese called the street *Lam Chan Ah,* as there were swampy rice-fields here in the early days of Penang. Some of the oldest shophouses look as if they were built under primitive, marshy conditions. Even now, the low-lying areas are flooded during high tides and heavy rains.

Carnarvon Lane was part of the Malay *kampong,* and the Chinese still call it *Kam Kong Lai.*

Above, shops selling religious paraphernalia. Below, primitive shophouses originally built on swampy land, now undertakers' row. (demolished)

an order later discovered to be invalid because Khoo Poh was already a naturalised British subject. Thus free from restraint, Khoo Poh continued to prosper until his death in 1892.

In 1921, the bungalow became the premises of the youth club called *Li Teik Seah,* which takes its name "Perenially Fresh" from the *I Ching.* True to its name, it has given birth to seven schools altogether (now located at Macallum Street Ghaut).

LI TEIK SEAH BUILDING

The Red Flag-Khian Teik alliance was strengthened by marriage when Syed Alatas took the daughter of Khoo Tiang Poh as his second wife (see also Syed Alatas Mansion, Armenian Street). Syed Alatas' second home was a gift from his father-in-law.

Khoo Tiang Poh alias Khoo Poh, a wealthy pepper trader and a close associate of the Achehnese community, lived in a large house at the junction of Acheen Street and Carnarvon Street (formerly the Bangkok Hotel, now a vacant site).

The Commission of Enquiry into the Penang Riots of 1867 named Khoo Poh and his clansman Khoo Thean Teik chief instigators of the gang war (see also Cannon Square).

Khoo Poh was sentenced to deportation -

SEH TEOH KONGSI

The Teoh surname clan association was founded in 1895 by Cheong Fatt Tze and others (see also Leith Street). The nearby Hong Kong Street has been renamed Cheong Fatt Tze Road only recently, after the original Cheong Fatt Tze Road was erased by the Komtar development.

Above, Syed Alatas' second home, now Li Teik Seah premises. Below, the entrance to the Seh Teoh Kongsi.

CHE EM LANE

In Francis Light's account of brick buildings on the island in 1793, *Chee Eam Chinaman* was named as the largest Chinese owner with three shophouses worth a total of 2,700 Spanish Dollars.

The pioneer settler Che Em alias Cheah Yam later became founder of the Cheah Kongsi (see also Armenian Street).

He probably lived and owned properties along the earliest section of China Street, with a second frontage on the narrow Che Em Lane - the first street in George Town to be named after a non-European personality.

In the vicinity of Penang's wet markets there is usually a small lane used by the poulterers for slaughtering chickens. In the late 19th century, Che Em Lane served as the poultry section of the nearby market, hence the Tamil name *Koli Kadai Sandhu*.

CHEAPSIDE

The narrow alley off Chulia Street takes its name after London's flea market area of the same name. Penang's version only specialises in hardware and locks.

CHINA STREET

China Street is the street of Penang's earliest Chinese traders. The Chinese have called it *Tua Kay* (Main Street) since it was laid out by Francis Light.

The trading street was established by the pioneer settler Koh Lay Huan, who presented Light with a fishing net on 18th July 1786, the day after Light's men made their landing on the island's northeastern cape.

Koh Lay Huan alias Che Kay alias Che Wan came from Kuala Muda, Kedah, bringing five hundred Chinese men, women and children from Kedah to settle in Penang.

He was said to have been an educated Chinese who rebelled against the Manchu government and so could not return to China. Francis Light appointed him Kapitan China of Penang the following year.

Lay Huan was instrumental in introducing pepper cultivation to Penang (see also Ayer Itam). He died in 1826 and his magnificent tomb can still be seen in the Batu Lanchang cemetery. His tomb was described by Holman, a famous blind person who travelled round the world in the 1840s.

Koh Lay Huan was the patriarch of a highly illustrious family. His son accompa-

---

Below, key-making at Cheapside. Above, a frieze from an early elite shophouse on China Street.

nied Stamford Raffles on the mission to found Singapore in 1819. His grandson Koh Seang Tat was a Municipal Commissioner (see also Light Street) as was his sixth generation descendant the late Koh Sin Hock.

Another grandson Koh Seang Tek (after whom Seang Tek Road is named) started an early ice factory on Penang Street. He was the father of Dr. Koh Leap Teng, the second Chinese Queen's Scholar from Penang and the first western-trained Chinese doctor to practice in Penang.

Koh Lay Huan lived in a brick shophouse in the section of China Street between Beach and Penang Streets. The mid-19th century Ghee Hin leader Ho Ghi Siu who was a biscuit-maker also had his shop on China Street. In the late 19th century, two outstanding figures who were born or grew up in China Street were Eu Tong Sen and Wu Lien Teh; the first built an empire out of traditional Chinese medicine, and the second is remembered in Western medicine as the man who defeated the Manchurian Plague.

George Town's oldest "elite shophouses" or townhouses are found along China Street - several have a second front along Che Em Lane - and elsewhere in the historic centre.

The residences-cum-stores of the early

Above left, the vista of the Goddess of Mercy Temple on Pitt Street. Above right, detail of an old shop sign along China Street. Below left, the elite section of China Street, near Beach Street. Below right, detail of gable.

Chinese merchants were highly individualistic buildings of fine quality decoration, capped by tall, ornate gables. Some appear to be two or more shophouses, but are internally connected and have common courtyards. The front courtyard sometimes featured a rock garden.

To distinguish these elite shophouses, their stature and decoration must be compared with other shophouses from the same period, as later buildings generally tend to be taller and more ornate.

Until the late 19th century, the wealthy Chinese lived exclusively in these "elite shophouses". Koh Seang Tat and his partner Foo Tye Sin who moved out to live in bungalows on Light Street in the 1860s were in fact life-style pioneers (see also Light Street).

China Street leads from the waterfront straight to the Goddess of Mercy Temple on Pitt Street. The splendid vista is usually missed by the one-way traffic in the opposite direction, but can however be enjoyed from one of the many pleasant coffeeshops between King and Queen Streets.

Cheng Ho Seah

This elite shophouse has a High Straits Eclectic-style facade from around the turn of the century (see also Penang Street). It was formerly the base of the Cheng Ho Seah, an association dedicated to the Snake Temple deity Chor Soo Kong. The association has since moved to the Tua Pek Kong Temple (see also Armenian Street).

Chettiar Lodge

The *Nagara Viduthi* (City Lodge), established in 1937, is a lodge of the Chettiar community, converted from a former Chinese residence. Chettiar immigrants used such lodges in both the port of departure and port of entry.

Above, the former Cheng Ho Seah. Below left, detail of innovative Chinese shophouse cornice decoration using European ceramic colours. Below right, the Chettiar lodge with typical Indian doors and wall tiles.

CHINA STREET GHAUT

WISMA KASTAM

The Customs Building, formerly the Malayan Railway Building, is part of a handsome ensemble comprising early 20th century trading offices and warehouses.

The Malayan Railway Building was often referred to as "the only railway station without a rail". Instead of platforms or trains, it had administrative offices, a ticketing booth and a Railway Restaurant with Bar & Grill.

Passengers bought their tickets at the Penang Railway Station, walked to the Railway Jetty at the end of China Street Ghaut, and boarded the Railway Ferry Steamers to Butterworth to catch the train. Fares to and from Penang were inclusive of the ferry ride.

When built in 1907, the Malayan Railway Building marked the timely completion of the FMS Railway which efficiently brought out tin and crops from the Federated Malay States for export.

Articulated on three sides, it used to stand prominently at the edge of the once-bustling pier. The clocktower greeted those who approached the island by sea, or alternatively, presented the last sight of George Town for those who sailed away.

CHOWRASTA ROAD

The Urdu word *Chowrasta* means "Four Cross Roads". In the 19th century, the Chowrasta Lines and prison were located along Penang Road.

The present-day Chowrasta Market is placed squarely within Chowrasta Street, Tamil Street, Kuala Kangsar Road and Penang Road.

This market, which the Chinese still call *Kelinga Ban San* (Indian Market), used to be dominated by Tamil Muslim petty traders.

About half a dozen South Indian food stalls on Tamil Street remain open all night to cater to the market workers.

The Malayan Railway building with clocktower. At the Beach Street end is Georgetown Dispensary, a wonderful corner building designed by Swan & McLaren in 1923.

CHULIA STREET

The most interesting street to explore on foot is Chulia Street, which has retained its multi-cultural character, traditional trades and crafts, antique architecture and living historic community.

South Indian Muslims came to early Penang in such great numbers that they soon overran "Malabar Street" laid out by Light and extended it to Penang Road. The name was quickly changed to "Chulia Street" in view of the fact that the majority of traders came from Tanjore and to a lesser extent from Ramnad, both districts in Tamil Nadu.

The Chinese called the western section *Gu Kan Tang* (Cattle-Pen Street), as livestock was kept there by the Indians. The original Indian neighbourhood formerly included the adjoining Argyll Road and Kampong Malabar.

This rapid development resulted in a haphazard layout of residential alleys with large monsoon gutters for draining the once swampy area. Much of the street's early 19th century features have survived.

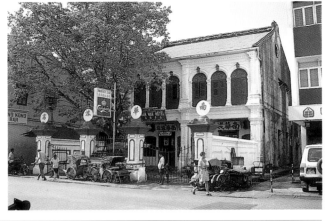

Above, Penang's famous low-budget tourist street. Below, a residence converted into a hotel - on the west side is a monsoon drain which runs from Muntri Street to Campbell Street, on the east side is "Lau Fook Chye Alley".

No other street has such a rich collection of urban Muslim buildings. The Kapitan Kling Mosque (circa 1800) originally had its entrance at Chulia Street. The Noordin Tomb (mid-19th century) and the Nagore shrine (circa 1800) are also jewels of South Indian Muslim architecture.

A number of other smaller Indian Muslim shrines and mosques date back to the early chapter of Penang's history - Mesjid Abdul Kader Alimshah (founded early 1800s, tomb from 1811, present mosque from 1952), Keramat Shaik Nathersah (died 1845) and the burial ground along Jalan Masjid (off Lebuh Chulia) and several others which have been modernized or are no longer extant. Shaik Nathersah endowed the "Hasharah Khana" along Jalan Masjid for Awal Muharram celebrations and it became the birthplace of one of Penang's most important performing traditions, the Boria.

The Dahudi Bohra Mosque founded in the 1910s is also housed in an early bungalow. It is attended mainly by the Gujerati Muslim community in Penang.

It also has valuable examples of the first Anglo-Indian masonry bungalows dating from the turn of the 19th century, the same period as Suffolk House. The two examples featured here, Yen Ching Hotel and Chung King Hotel, are Georgian in their symmetry and feature paired Roman columns and have semi-hipped roofs. Specimens of this particular domestic architecture seem to be found only in George Town, and not in other urban areas in the country.

Examples of these early masonry bungalows and their half-masonry, half-timber variants survive behind the street-fronting shophouses; the latter were developed at least some half a century later. Chinese shopkeepers moved into Chulia Street in the late 19th century, when the Indian Muslim trading community declined.

Above, early 19th century bungalows tucked behind late 19th century shophouses - next to Eng Aun Hotel (with the red roof) is the Dahudi Bohra Mosque, and across the road is the Swiss Hotel. Below, Chungking Hotel.

At the beginning of the twentieth century, many old buildings were converted into budget hotels, which first catered mainly to domestic and Asian tourists, and then from the 1960s increasingly to European low-budget travellers.

Internationally known as a budget tourist strip today, economy travel agencies, antique shops and tourist cafes have proliferated along Chulia Street in the last few years. Budget heritage hotels like Eng Aun Hotel and Tye Ann Hotel, which also provide coffeeshop-style breakfasts, are all listed in the regular backpackers' guides. Eng Aun hotel once belonged to Shaik Dawood Maricar bin Mohamed Sadak Maricar, a trustee of the Nagore Shrine, who first organised the Maulud Nabi flag festivals in Penang.

The most internationally well-known is the Swiss Hotel, where the German tourist Frank Forster was arrested in the mid-1980s. He was brought to trial in Malaysia for drug-trafficking but finally acquitted. The courtcase

was televised worldwide. Notwithstanding the incident, the Chulia Street hotels remain exceedingly popular with law-abiding tourists.

Sailors who come into town head straight for the Hong Kong Bar and other night spots. Chulia Street today has a seedy reputation among locals as a red light area. However, it should be emphasized that the low-budget brothels cater mainly to sailors, domestic tourists and locals.

Admittedly, the street could do with some cleaning up, but the dark appearance of the buildings is not so much the result of nefarious activities, historic or contemporary, as of the soot left by the city buses.

Above left, behind the shophouses is 'Cheyen House', once used as a lodge for Kadaiyanallur immigrants (now demolished). Above right, detail of the Dahudi Bohra Mosque, Below, Eng Aun Hotel, a former Muslim mansion.

YEN KENG HOTEL

Yen Keng is the old name for Peking. The hotel catered to travelling tradesmen who came out to Penang in large numbers during China's turbulent period in the late 19th and early 20th centuries.

Originally an early 19th century Anglo-Indian bungalow, this was one of the earliest buildings along Chulia Street to be adapted into a hotel. A gate and wall were added in front and a Chinese courtyard was created at the back.

JAPANESE CLUB

This early Indo-Malay house was reportedly used as a *Jit-Pun-A Kong Kwan* (Japanese Club) until 1914, when the present tenants moved in. It is set back from the street front, and located in an area that was known for Japanese geisha houses at the turn of the century (see also Cintra Street).

Above, the Anglo-Indian bungalow which became the Yen Ching Hotel. Below, the Japanese Club building - some of the original timber transom screens have been replaced with oriental latticework.

NAGORE SHRINE

This is the earliest Indian Muslim shrine in Penang which survives in its original condition. It is located on the original section of Chulia Street laid out by Light.

The Nagore Shrine was built in the early 1800s as a memorial to Syed Shahul Hamid, the famous 13th century Muslim Saint of Nagore, who has a whole religious complex dedicated to him in Nagore.

The tradition of the city saint was brought to Penang by the Tamil Muslim traders from Tanjore. Feast days are still observed with flag-raising and distribution of food, but minus the flag parades of prewar days.

The side wall of the shrine has a built-in arcade - two alcoves are occupied by makers of the *songkok* (Muslim headwear). The shrine formerly had a well on King Street. A pair of dingy-looking neighbouring shophouses survive from the early 19th century.

Above, the Nagore Shrine. Middle, the shrine sign. Below, the section of Chulia Street near Beach Street which the Chinese call "Noordin Street", as here were formerly a row of shops owned by M.M. Noordin and his sons.

NOORDIN FAMILY TOMB

Mohamed Merican Noordin alias M. M. Noordin, who came to Penang around 1820, succeeded Kapitan Kling as the most prominent Chulia in Penang.

The Noordins ran a fleet of ships that called at the ports along the Straits of Malacca, Burma, China, India, the Middle East and Europe, trading in spices and other commodities, as well as transporting immigrants and pilgrims.

Noordin contributed generously towards the cost of laying down pipes from the Waterfall for the town's water supply and was thus one of the first Muslims to be made a Municipal Commissioner and a Justice of the Peace.

He took wives of various origins, including a European wife, and several of his sons followed his example. M. M. Noordin had the family tomb built by Indian masons for his mother, and was himself buried there after 1870. The facade was added at the turn of the century.

The vestibule of the tomb accommodated one of the first schools for the Muslim community, with which he endowed "for the learning of English, Hindoostanee, Malay, Tamil, Malabar, and the Alkoran. Twenty dollars per month".

The surrounding buildings in the tomb area caught fire in early 1993, but the tomb itself was unharmed.

Above, the arabesque decorations on the facade of the Noordin Family Tomb. Below left, the arches and columns are constructed from hand-cut bricks. Below right, the burial ground surrounded by a cloister.

PENANG TEOCHEW ASSOCIATION

Many of the planters who developed Province Wellesley belong to the Teochew dialect group. This temple was founded here in the early 19th century, and built in 1870.

In the 1930s the temple was renovated and the Teochew Merchant's Association was added next door, which served as the early premises of the Han Chiang School.

YEOH KONGSI

When it was founded in 1836, the Yeoh Kongsi stood on the waterfront and had its own clan jetty (see also Weld Quay). From the prayer hall on the upper floor of the double-storey temple, the clansmen had a clear view of the sea.

It is closely affiliated to the Yeoh Kongsi in Rangoon, as the members of both associations comprise descendants from the same clan village in Hokkien province, China.

Above, an informal unnamed alley off Chulia Street which the residents call Lau Fook Chye Hang. Below, the beautifully painted doors of the Penang Teochew Association.

UNITED ASSOCIATION OF CANTONESE DISTRICTS

The *Ng Fook Tong* (Five Luck Villa) founded in 1819 was one of the earliest Chinese schools in this country. The present association building dates from 1898 and originally served as a night school (see also Chung Keng Kwee Temple, Church Street).

CENTRAL FIRE STATION

The police doubled as George Town's fire-fighters until 1909, when the newly-formed Fire Brigade of 28 trained men took over. A sub-station opened in Penang Road that year, followed by the Central Fire Station at Chulia Street Ghaut, since renamed the Beach Street Fire Station.

Above, the roof decoration of the United Cantonese Association building. Middle, the Central Fire Station, since refurbished. Below, the Yeoh Kongsi with the original tiled forecourt.

CHURCH STREET

Here was the first church of the Portuguese Eurasians, sometimes referred to as the "Portuguese Church" in the old documents (see also also Bishop Street).

By the early 19th century, the Eurasians had already moved their church out to Farquhar Street, and Church Street in the town centre was taken over by commerce.

Today, Church Street is still remembered as *Ghee Hin Kay* because the Ghee Hin secret society was based there for almost a century - and in spite of the fact that the premises were subsequently taken over by the leader of the Hai San secret society.

CHUNG KENG KWEE TEMPLE, HAI KEE CHAN OFFICE & RESIDENCE

Chung Keng Kwee led the Hai San secret society throughout the years of the protracted tin wars with the Ghee Hin.

The *Hai San* (Sea Mountain) society was then dominated by Hakka members - especially after the early 1860s when its ranks were swelled by Hakka rebels who fled China when the Taiping Rebellion was crushed.

As a result of the Pangkor Engagement of 1874, Chung Keng Kwee was appointed Kapitan China to sit on the Perak State Council along with two Ghee Hin leaders (see also Pangkor Road).

Above left, the Dragon King building's second frontage on Church Street. Below, early 19th century Anglo-Indian shophouses; notice the fake fanlights. Above right, gilded screen in the Chung Keng Kwee Temple.

He died in 1901, and his grand tomb can still be seen at Mount Erskine. He was succeeded by his western-educated son, Chung Thye Pin, who expanded the family's mining business and served as the country's last Kapitan China.

Chung Keng Kwee alias Keng Kooi alias Ah Quee has two streets named after him in Penang (see also Ah Quee Street). His donations to the war and flood relief funds in China bought him the title Mandarin of Second Rank.

The family mansions included the former Shanghai Hotel and the Relau Villa with a freshwater swimming pool (still extant), and several more in Perak, Hong Kong and China. A saying about Chung Keng Kwee goes that "others may equal him in wealth, but not in mansions".

The Chung Keng Kwee temple and mansion at Church Street form an ensemble of

Above, the historic ensemble of the temple and office-cum-residence. The four-storey pavilion behind belongs to an elite shophouse facing China Street. Below right, the cast iron balcony.

great historic importance to the histories of Penang and Perak.

In 1893, shortly after the prohibition of secret societies, Keng Kwee took over two properties in Church Street.

The first was the headquarters of the rival Ghee Hin, where the old secret society had been based since the early 19th century (see also Rope Walk).

The second was the

premises of an early Chinese school, the *Goh Hock Tong* (Five Luck Villa). Keng Kwee compensated the school with a site on Chulia Street (see also United Cantonese Association, Chulia Street).

On the former Ghee Hin site, he built a residence-cum-office called *Hai Kee Chan* (Sea Remembrance Store). This Straits Eclectic town mansion is uniquely laid out, with a five-foot way along the facade and several large courtyards.

Interior fittings include a grand staircase, stencilled window panes, a rock fountain and Victorian cast iron columns at the central courtyard and balcony. A beautifully woodcarved panel from the upper floor is displayed in the State Museum.

On the former Goh Hock Tong site, Keng Kwee built a private temple which served as an ancestral hall and family school. The old Kapitan made a life-sized statue of himself for family worship. The temple's ornate roof decorations, gilded woodcarvings and ceramic sculptured tableaux are of the finest Cantonese craftsmanship.

The complicated layout of the temple premises include several narrow passages and walled courtyards. Behind the ancestral hall,

Above, the temple set back with a granite forecourt. Below, the ancestral altar, with the life-size statue of Chung Keng Kwee behind the altar table.

in a secluded courtyard accessible only through the narrow eastern passageway, is an ancient well.

Here the Ghee Hin disposed of some of their rivals from the Tua Pek Kong society, and later the Hai San did the same with Ghee Hin victims. Due to its bloody past, the well has since been covered up so that the spirits can finally rest.

CINTRA STREET

Cintra is a port in Portugal, and Cintra Street recalls a time when Eurasians lived and traded here in the 19th century.

Before 1900, there were already Japanese geisha houses in the section between Campbell and Chulia Street, which was called *Je-Pun Kay*. Then in the early 20th century, Japanese camera shops, which were suspected to have been a cover for spying operations, sprouted up along Malabar and Cintra Streets.

The street offers good food in a number of old-fashioned Cantonese coffeeshops such as *Tai Tong* and *Foo Heong*.

People's Court was Penang's first government low-cost housing development project. It was built by the City Council in 1961.

Above, the ceramic sculpture decorations, unique in the country. Below, the temple interior with granite courtyard and columns.

The threat to the building gave rise to Penang's first widely-publicized conservation protest in the mid-1980s, which however did not save it from demolition.

There is nonetheless another College-General building which survives from the early 1800s. It is part of *Mariophile* in Tanjung Bungah, beautifully sited on St. John's Hill (next to Mount Miriam).

COLLEGE SQUARE

The French Catholic mission moved from Burma to Penang in 1803, followed by the College-General three years later.

The "Seminary of the Holy Angels", better known as *College-General,* was founded in Ayuthia in 1660. Over the next century, the seminary moved its base to Hondat in Cambodia and then to Pondicherry in India.

The regional seminary served to train teachers for the mission in Siam, Cochin-China, India, China, Japan, and later Burma and Malaya. It closed down in 1782 due to the lack of a suitable base, and reopened in 1806 in Pulau Tikus, Penang.

The College-General compex at Kelawai Road was built in 1810 (hence the adjacent College Square named after it).

The Anglo-Indian bungalow was formerly used as a hill retreat. This important building stands in highly original condition, guarded by two old cannons.

The adjacent Chapel, also from the early 19th century, contains relics from missionary saints who died in Vietnam.

In 1984, the College-General moved back to *Mariophile,* and the new seminary buildings are located at the foot of the hill, with the entrance from Jalan Chengai (off Jalan Gajah).

Above, College Square, off Kelawai Road. Below, an early 19th century Anglo-Indian bungalow in highly original condition - the College-General building at Mariophile on St. John's Hill, guarded by a pair of cannons.

80

DATO KRAMAT ROAD

The earliest decent road to the interior led along Dato Kramat Road to the Waterfall; at this junction where it veers off towards Waterfall Road, Dato Kramat Road ends and Ayer Itam Road begins.

Originally, it was the road to the Dato Kramat village - a settlement by the Pinang River established before Light's arrival. It was probably with this community that the early Tamils traded for betel-nut, giving the island its name *Pulau Pinang*.

In the early 18th century, the community's leader was Dato Kramat, a Muslim ascetic of Tamil and possibly Acehnese origin (see also Perak Road).

Keramat is an Arabic word for a holy person or place. In Penang, it commonly refers to the shrine or tomb of a Muslim saint, visited by those who ask for favours and intercession.

In the 19th century, the area around Dato Kramat Road was famous for its orange groves, hence the Malay Name *Kebun Limau* and the Hokkien name *Kam Mah Hui*.

HAJI KASSIM MOSQUE

In the early years, Malay and Acehnese traders sailed up the Pinang River to trade with the villages in the interior.

At the beginning of the 19th century, the community was led by Haji Kassim, a religious teacher from Aceh. He founded the Mesjid Haji Kassim before 1840.

The village which developed around a jetty on the Pinang River was known as *Pengkalan Haji Kassim*.

After his death, a mausoleum was built to his memory and the village has since been known as *Kampong Makam*.

BROWN MEMORIAL

Dato Kramat Padang, a 12-acre playing field, was formerly a landscaped park known as Brown Gardens. A memorial to David Brown, who donated the land to the municipality, stands at one corner, moved from its former site in the middle of the field.

David Brown, who studied law in Edinburgh, came on an adventure to Penang. Here he joined his countryman James Scott, previously Light's trading partner. Much of Scott's business passed on to his junior partner and upon the former's death, Brown became the largest landowner on the island.

As merchants and owners of large plantations, the Scottish were the most important group of European settlers in early Penang.

Brown became the doyen of European planters and the patriarch of the famous

A corner coffeeshop at the junction of Dato Kramat Road and Perak Road.

Brown family of Glugor (see also Glugor Road). His first wife was a local woman called *Nonia Ennui,* and his second wife was a Malay woman called *Inghoo.*

He used his great influence in the settlement to the advantage of the non-European community, and donated much land to the public, including the site of the Snake Temple and the Sungai Glugor Mosque. Upon his death in 1821, his memorial was raised by public subscription.

Until the mid-19th century, the perma-

nent "European" community of Penang largely comprised descendants of those early settlers who had taken local wives - Light, Scott, Brown and Logan being the most prominent among them.

It was only after the advent of the steamship and the opening of the Suez canal, which made voyages shorter and safer, that European women also came to the Straits Settlements in significant numbers.

Intermarriages between the Europeans and the locals became less common, a trend which inevitably contributed to the making of a more rigid class society during the heyday of the British Empire.

DATUK KERAMAT SMELTING

This international tin smelting concern began as *Seng Kee Tin Smelting Works* in 1897. The founder was Lee Chin Ho, the first Chinese smelter to adopt the use of European reverberatory furnaces.

Tin was transferred from the company's mines at Gopeng, Perak, and also from the mines of South Thailand and smelted into ingots for re-export.

Above, a dragon weaving its way through Dato Kramat Road during the Penang on Parade festival. Below, the memorial to Brown in the centre of a hawker complex at one corner of the Dato Kramat playing field.

In 1907, the company was floated as Eastern Smelting, a limited liability company with a capital of one and a half million dollars, attracting North Malaya's largest tin magnates to its board, including the Khaw family (see also Koe Guan Office, Beach Street).

Chin Ho lived in Birch House, built in 1908, while his relatives and workers lived in the surrounding rowhouses in Chin Ho Square. Now used as the company offices, Birch House was given a modern facade after the war. The back door conveniently leads to the tin-smelting works proper.

On the roof of Birch House is a small figurine of a Tang dynasty general which Chin Ho installed to ward off influences from the Shiva Temple opposite. Subsequent managements have decided to retain this charm.

Located in the vicinity of the old *Kampong Jawa* village, the tin works conveniently employed Javanese labour. When the factory expanded, more workers were brought in from Java, and the latter extended the neighbourhood, setting up the *Kampong Jawa Baru* next to the *Kampong Jawa Lama*.

PENANG HINDU SABAH

The British engaged educated Indians from Madras to fill the civil service and clerical jobs in trading companies. Among the early recruits were printing workers brought to this country to run the Pinang Gazette Press.

In 1912, a group of printing workers formed the Pinang Hindu Sabah for the "upliftment" of the general Hindu community.

The driving force behind its founding was N. Nadeson Pillai, the superintendent of the Pinang Gazette Press for nearly forty years and the first Hindu Justice of the Peace.

DOWNING STREET

As in London, Downing Street in George Town was the street of Government. The grand administrative complex at King Edward Place and Downing Street was the target of Japanese bombing during the Second World War which left only one building intact.

The Government Offices were erected in several stages from 1889. The first block housed the Resident Councillor's Office, the Audit Office, the Public Works Department, the Marine Department and the Harbour Master's Office. It was extended with a western wing for the Land Office and an eastern wing for the Post Office.

In addition, there were separate buildings housing the Chinese Protectorate and the Indian Immigration Depot to process the thousands of immigrants that came through this port of call each year.

The last extension to the complex was erected after 1907 and this block escaped the bombs. Recently refurbished, it now accommodates the offices of the State Religious Council and a *syariah* court.

The international-style Bangunan Tuanku Syed Putra was erected as the seat of the State Government around 1960.

The recently renovated Religious Council building at Downing Street.

DRURY LANE

Drury Lane was Penang's West End. The locals call it *Sin Hi Tai* (New Theatre), while the ajdoining Kuala Kangsar Road was "Bangsawan Street".

The theatre, which has since been replaced by a modern cinema, was rented by the Chinese for their opera and the Malays for their *Bangsawan* (see also Aboo Siti Lane).

ESPLANADE ROAD

The Fort Cornwallis, as is typical of the Indian forts, had its own field for military practice, clearly separating the base from civilian areas (see also Light Street). As the defence function of the fort became less plausible, the Esplanade was increasingly used for recreational purposes.

The *Padang* had several buildings on it. Second World War bombs destroyed the Penang Sports Club (Cricket Section) and the Penang Recreation Club for Eurasians. There were two Victorian cast iron pavilions - the Vermont Memorial and the Municipal Band Stand - as well as ornate benches and lamp posts.

Indeed, most of the iron structures and fittings so common in prewar Penang, including balustrades and fences, were removed during the Japanese occupation. The scrap metal was recycled into bullets.

The Town Hall was built in 1883, with an assembly hall, a ballroom and a library. The functions were more social than administrative, and for that the Chinese called it the *Ang Mo Kong Kuan* (European Club).

From 1890 to 1954, the Town Hall maintained a Town Band made up of Filipino musicians. The Manila Band subsidized itself by performing at clubs, hotels and private

The Municipal Council buildings on the old esplanade. The grand ballroom on the first floor of the Town Hall was used as the courthouse scene in the movie 'Anna & The King'.

parties. They held open-air performances at the band stands at the Esplanade and the Penang Botanic Gardens.

The City Hall was built at a cost of 100,000 Straits Dollars and incorporated ironwork from Europe. It opened in 1906, being one of the first buildings to be completely fitted with electric lights and fans (see also Huttenbach Godowns).

The Esplanade today features a Municipal hawker centre and a popular waterfront promenade.

Here are two reminders of the First World War - a cenotaph with brass relief plates, and a red buoy in the middle of the sea which marks the spot where the Russian ship *Zemschug* was sunk by the German cruise ship *Emden*.

The *Emden* had sailed

into port with a fourth funnel made of burlap, disguising itself as the HMS Yarmouth which was expected to call (see also Western Road).

In prewar days, the Esplanade was the venue for a romantic Straits Chinese tradition. Nyonya maidens were paraded in trishaws and buggies on Chap Goh Meh, the fifteenth night of Chinese New Year, to be selected by prospective suitors. The latter noted down the number of their fair lady's carriage and gave it to the town matchmaker the next day for further investigation.

On this full moon night, maidens cast oranges into the sea wishing for good husbands, according to the old rhyme "throw oranges, and get a good husband". *Dondang Sayang* balladeers set the mood for love at first sight.

Above, the City Hall, where Penang's twenty-four Municipal Councillors meet regularly in the Council Chambers. Below, detail from the cenotaph.

FARQUHAR STREET

During his term (1804-1805) as Lieutenant-Governor of Penang, Robert Townsend Farquhar* recommended the destruction of the fort and city of Malacca.

The Dutch colony had temporarily come under the East India Company administration in Penang during the Napoleonic Wars, and Farquhar was anxious to destroy Malacca before the Dutch returned.

The culturally enlightened Raffles who arrived in 1805 took a preservationist stand out of respect for the ancient city, but only managed to stop the demolition of *A Famosa* in its final stages, when all that was left was the *Porta De Santiago*.

On the other hand, Farquhar also had ambitions to be the greatest builder of early Penang. During his administration, the aqueduct and Government House were constructed, and the defences of Fort Cornwallis enlarged.

The four-mile long aqueduct was a monumental effort which required the labour of several hundred convicts (see also Waterfall Road). The "open brick drain" ran from the Waterfall along Burmah Road to a small reservoir at the present site of the E & O Hotel. Ships stopped here at "Sweet Water Bay" to refill with fresh water from the Penang hills.

Farquhar's plan to recover the cost of the aqueduct from selling the water was however impracticable, for the Company's ships could not be charged and the public already enjoyed free water from the Town Well.

When Penang was elevated to a Presidency, Farquhar was recalled to India; he later became Governor of Mauritius.

Farquhar was disparaged by his successor Phillip Dundas for having run the government into great debt with his extravagant building schemes. However, even Farquhar's detractors among the new government had to admit that they enjoyed the comforts of the vastly improved facilities.

Farquhar Street was part of the great civic park which featured the Anglican and the Catholic churches, and the cradle of four of Penang's greatest English-medium schools - the Penang Free School (founded 1816), Convent Light Street (founded 1852), St. Xavier's Institution (La Sallean Brothers, founded 1852) and St. George's Girls' School (Anglican Mission, founded 1885).

St. Xavier's Institution was completely rebuilt after the former building, used as a Japanese naval base, was destroyed by Al-

---

* Not to be confused with his contemporary, Major William Farquhar of Malacca and Singapore.

lied Bombs dropped from B-29's toward the end of the Second World War.

Today, Farquhar Street is divided into two one-way lanes. The E & O Hotel facade can be much better appreciated if approached from an easterly direction. Next to the hotel is a bungalow and stables from 1888, formerly housing St. George's Girls' School.

St. George's Church

Two great men were involved in building St. George's Church, the earliest Anglican church in the region. The first was Reverend R.S. Hutchings, then Colonial Chaplain, who was also the driving force behind the establishment of the Penang Free School. The second was Captain Robert N. Smith of Madras Engineers, who painted the famous early views of Penang.

The marriage in 1818 of W.E. Phillips to Janet Bannerman, daughter of Colonel J.A. Bannerman, was the first to be solemnized in the new church. Incidentally, the building of the church was started during Phillips' term as Governor in 1817 and completed during Bannerman's, the next year (see also Suffolk House).

The church building cost 60,000 Spanish Dollars. The original Madras-style flat roof was unsuited to the climate, and was thus changed to a pitched roof in 1864. During the Second World War, the church structure was only slightly damaged but the interior was badly looted.

The building was later restored and almost all the furnishings replaced - the only original items are the font and the bishop's chair. There are also a number of memorial tablets laid in the church walls and floor.

The Greek temple in the grounds is a monument to Francis Light, inscribed,

In his capacity as Governor the settlers and natives were greatly attached to him and by his death had to deplore the loss of one who watched over their interests and cares as a father.

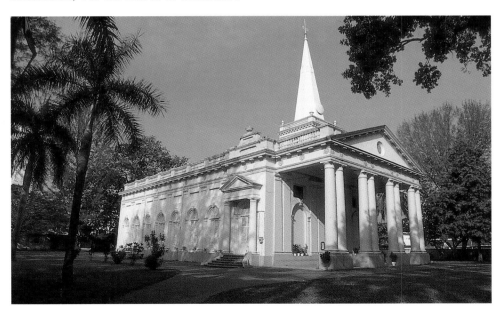

Opposite page, Light's Monument serves as an introduction to early Penang. Above, St. George's Church, similar to the one in Madras.

The Church of England stood in the middle of the three-acre "Company's Square". Today, the view of the grand church edifice and its picturesque setting remains virtually unchanged.

FRANCIS LIGHT MEMORIAL

Captain Francis Light was born out of wedlock in Suffolk county in 1740. He was fathered by a certain nobleman named William Negus, but took his mother's name, Light. He met James Scott when both were young midshipmen with the Royal Navy.

In his twenties, Light went out to Madras and became master of *Speedwell.* He operated the country ship for the firm *Jourdain Sulivan & De Souza,* and traded between India, Aceh and the peninsula.

Light based himself in Phuket, where he had met the Portuguese Eurasian Martina Rozells. Together they set up a trading post in Kuala Kedah.

Penang was recommended by Light as early as 1771, but only in 1786 was the Governor-General of India interested enough to authorise him to negotiate with the Sultan of Kedah.

In his role as first Superintendent of the Prince of Wales Island, Light laid out the town, established the port and developed the island's agricultural base. To avoid any conflict of interest, he left his commercial inter-

ests to the management of his partner James Scott.

By 1793, Light owned "2 Dwelling Houses & Offices" worth 16,000 Spanish Dollars (see also Suffolk House, Ayer Itam and Leith Street Ghaut). Light also had a hill home and cultivated strawberries successfully on Strawberry Hill.

He died in 1794 and left behind four children which he had with Martina - Sarah, William, Lanoon and Lukey.

In 1836, fifty years after his father founded Penang, William Light, as first Surveyor-General of South Australia, sited and laid out Adelaide, which has often been acclaimed by city planners as one of the best planned cities in the world.

The Francis Light Memorial which stands outside the museum was modelled upon the features of William Light, as no picture of his father could be found.

The bronze statue was sculpted by F.J. Wilcoxson and cast at Burton's Foundry, Thames Ditton. The memorial was commissioned by the Municipal Council during the sesquicentenary celebrations of the founding of Penang in 1936.

In 1973, Penang and Adelaide were twinned. Tucked away for years, the statue of Francis Light that was made in William Light's likeness was brought back into public view in 1978 for the visit of the Premier of South Australia, Don Dunstan.

Francis Light's Memorial outside the Penang State Museum - like father, like son.

Penang State Museum

The Penang State Museum, which re-opened in 1998 after a major renovation, is today one of the best state museums in Malaysia. The art gallery, formerly housed in the same building, has moved to the Dewan Sri Pinang on Light Street to make more room for the museum displays.

The Museum at Farquhar Street first opened in 1965. The exhibits are organised according to Penang's communities, their customs and customes, historical places and streets of Penag, municipal history, historical episodes such as the Penang Riots and the Japanese Occupation, houses of worship and traditional trades. The historical paintings of Captain Robert Smith and the engravings of William Daniels are elegantly displayed.

The museum building was constructed for the Penang Free School, which moved to its present, much larger premises at Green Lane in 1927. The schoolhouse was designed as a symmetrical building but erected in two stages, as funds allowed - the half near St. George's Church in 1896 and the other half in 1906.

It is an interesting coincidence that Second World War bombs fell on one half, leaving only half a building today - reconstruction of the eastern wing would have a historical parallel in the way it was erected in the first place.

The Penang Free School was founded on October 21st, 1816, marking the 30th anniversary of Light's death. It was proposed and tirelessly promoted by Rev. Hutchings.

The English-medium school for boys was established in the tradition of a British Public School. For the next century and a half, it set the precedent and standards for English education in the country, and produced more than its fair share of Queen's Scholars.

Three original intentions of the Free School - the first to have a school for girls, the second to provide vernacular education in Malay and Tamil, and the third to provide vocational training - were abandoned after the first few years due to lack of response.

Besides raising funds and single-handedly setting up the educational system, the indefatigable Hutchings prepared a Malay dictionary, grammars of the Malay language, and translated the Old and New Testaments into Jawi.

Hutchings started a plantation of nutmeg and spice on the hill which he named Mount Elvira after his wife, and to which he and his family retreated to escape the ravages of tropical disease.

But he did not escape - in 1827 he died from fever after all, not improbably as a result of sheer overwork.

Free School, Penang

The State Museum & Art Gallery, Penang, housed in the remaining half of the old Penang Free School building.

ran the famous Strand in Rangoon, the Raffles in Singapore and the Crag Hotel on Penang Hill. The Crag was first promoted as a sanatorium then as a premier honeymoon resort.

In the 1920s, youngest brother Arshak Sarkies indulged in a flamboyant expansion and the construction of the Victory Wing (the western wing, since demolished).

When those accustomed to fine living suffered from the rubber crash in the 1930s, the E & O became a place for people to "Eat & Owe" - bankrupting the generous Arshak.

THE EASTERN & ORIENTAL HOTEL

The newly re-opened Eastern & Oriental Hotel once boasted the "Longest Sea Front of Any Hotel" and also acclaimed itself "The Premier Hotel East of Suez". Like the Raffles in Singapore, the Eastern & Oriental harks back to the days of planters, palms, ceiling fans and *stengahs*.

Among the famous visitors to the hotel were the author Somerset Maugham and the playwright Noel Coward, who came with his friend Lord Amherst.

The enterprise began in 1885 when the Sarkies brothers met the Khaw family in Bangkok and were invited by the latter to set up a hotel in Penang.

The Khaws put up two buildings, which were later combined into one establishment. The hotel has undergone extensive renovations throughout its history, and the oldest original section seems to be the ballroom from 1903.

The Sarkies brothers also

CATHEDRAL OF THE ASSUMPTION

The Eurasians from Kedah landed in Penang on the eve of the Feast of the Assumption in 1786, and so named their church in celebration of their deliverance (see also Bishop Street and Church Street).

Above, the choice of Somerset Maugham and Noel Coward. Below, the Cathedral on Farquhar Street.

The Church moved to Farquhar Street around 1802, and the Eurasian community with it. The present building was erected in 1860 and underwent extensive renovations in 1928, when the two wings were added.

In 1955, by a Decree of the Vatican, the Assumption Church became a Cathedral with a Bishop presiding at the services. The Cathedral has a pipe organ.

GLUGOR ROAD

This was the road to the Glugor plantations of David Brown in the early 19th century. Brown achieved great success in his experiments to cultivate clove and nutmeg. The Glugor House that he built was the subject of many early paintings (see also Brown Memorial, Datok Keramat Road).

The Glugor Estate gave permanent employment to a large number of Hindu estate workers and the historic plantation community survived until recently.

Several pill boxes can be seen along the main road - these were fortified bunkers made to accommodate six to seven people, built by the British in preparation for Japanese invasion.

The fruit of the Gelugor tree is the *assam gelugor,* a tamarind used in local curries.

BATU UBAN MOSQUE

Even before 1786, a member of the Minangkabau royal family in Sumatra had founded a settlement at Batu Uban with the permission of the Sultan of Kedah.

A survey by Light found no less than 15 original inhabitants among the settlers who cleared this area for planting fruit trees, coconut and sugarcane.

Nakhoda Intan Ibn Al-marhum Nam Tungku Patis Batang is believed to have founded the Batu Uban Mosque in 1734. An old mosque structure survives, obscured by modern additions. It is located at the end of Jalan Masjid in the Batu Uban village, off Glugor Road.

Near the mosque entrance is a well which Nakhoda Intan sunk into a rock. The founder's tomb is regarded as a saint's shrine *(keramat).*

In prewar days, the mosque and tomb was a site of pilgrimage for Muslims from all over the country who came to feast *(kenduri)* and perform ritual bathing *(mandi safar)* on the saint's feast days.

GREEN LANE

Green Lane has been renamed Jalan Mesjid Negeri after the State Mosque was built in 1980. It was designed by a Filipino architect.

Penang's first suburbs for the local middle-class were created in the 1970s at Green Lane, and have since been extended to Island Glades and Minden Heights.

It was not that long ago that the road was literally a "green lane" passing through the countryside.

The first expression of Green awareness in Penang harks back to the early 1980s when the mature roadside trees of Green Lane came under threat.

The City's traffic engineers planned to widen the road to create a four-lane highway; the public raised hue and cry to save the Angsana trees. The compromise was to allow the highway to curve gracefully and to accommodate one row on the central divider.

GURNEY DRIVE

Living in a historic resort, a favourite pastime among Penangites is to*makan angin* (literally, "eating the breeze"). Pedestrians enjoy their morning strolls and after-dinner walks along the promenades and motorists enjoy their leisure drives along the tree-lined suburban roads.

The former north beach front was lined with casuarinas, coconut trees and holiday bungalows. Then North Beach (now known as Gurney Drive) was created, which became instantly popular with the first generation of driving enthusiasts.

The young motorists created a ritual of driving into Gurney Drive on New Year's Eve and honking their cars at the stroke of midnight. As the number of cars on the road have increased, the year traditionally begins and ends with the experience of a gigantic traffic jam.

Some holiday bungalows have been converted to cafes for seaside dining. The two-mile promenade used to be lined with hawkers, until the latter were relocated to the Municipal Hawker Centre.

Gurney Drive was the venue for the dragon boat races until recently. Land is currently being reclaimed on the western end.

North Beach was renamed Gurney Drive after Sir Henry Gurney who was ambushed and assassinated by the communists during the Emergency.

Above, the casuarina-lined promenade. Below, the arts-and-crafts style LWA Villa from 1926.

HUTTON LANE

Dr. Hutton was the earliest known doctor. He arrived with two assistants in 1805, when Penang became a Presidency.

The western end of Hutton Lane, near Larut Road, was the "Muslim Millionaire's Row". The present Savoy Hotel, renovated with a new facade in the late 19th century, was formerly the residence of Mohd. Ariff bin Mohamed Tajoodin, and then his son Wanchee Ariffin (see also Perak Road). Down the road were several homes belonging to the Ariff family. The residence of M.Z. Merican alias Teh Bunga, son-in-law of Mohd. Ariff has been well preserved.

Mohd. Ariff and his eldest son Wanchee Ariffin were great patrons of Boria. Wanchee kept the Boria minstrels singing for hours with generous tips, provoking complaints by the families of other households where the minstrels were expected to call.

Their ancestor was the distinguished pioneer Bapu Alauddin bin Meerah Hussein Lebai who as a representative of the Kedah Sultan accompanied Light to Penang.

JELUTONG ROAD

Before the Free Trade Zone, there was Jelutong. At the turn of the century, the area was a flourishing "factory suburb" of George Town. Some significant examples of factory buildings and godowns survive from this chapter of Penang's industrial history.

Jelutong's industries depended on the Pinang River for their water supply as well as waste disposal. After a century of dumping, the Pinang River today is reduced to a sprawling sewer. The dying river is no longer used as a waterway.

Jelutong was cleared by the Malays during Light's time. Their leader Nakhoda Kechil (literally "Little Captain") assisted Light in felling the trees at the site of Fort Cornwallis.

The original Jelutong village stood at the junction of Jelutong Road and Perak Road around the present Mesjid Nakhoda Kechil. The site of the mosque (since rebuilt) and surrounding burial ground was alienated to Nakhoda Kechil in 1797 and bequeathed by him to religious charity (waqf).

The village was named after the *Jelutong* tree which must have grown abundantly in this area. Malaysian pencils are mostly made from Jelutong wood.

Along the coast of Jelutong is a community of woodcutters and charcoal-makers at Bakau Road. Penang's charcoal is made from the wood of a mangrove known as

Above, a Straits Eclectic bungalow, formerly the residence of Teh Bunga, with the original circular driveway.

Phuah Hin Leong's eldest son Lim Cheng Teik, Khie Heng Bee Mills became one of the largest industrial concerns on the island (see also Phuah Hin Leong Road, and Limburg, Larut Road).

The mills were almost destroyed by a fire in 1918, then considered "the most disastrous in the annals of Penang", which took 22 hours to bring under control.

bakau, formerly collected in the vicinity but nowadays imported. The mangrove wood was also used in the early foundations for buildings erected in the swampy parts of George Town.

KHIE HENG BEE MILLS

The first industrial boom in the late 19th century saw the expansion of supporting industries such as food-processing. At the Khie Heng Bee factory, white rice was milled and boiled in large vats, loaded onto boats docked by the waterfront and delivered to the plantations to feed the labourers.

The Khie Heng Bee mills were spread out on five acres of land on both sides of Bridge Street. An "aerial tramway" or cable car was used to transport grain and copra between the drying area on the interior side and the mills and godowns on the waterfront.

The site was purchased from Khoo Tiang Poh (see also Carnarvon Street) by Phuah Hin Leong to expand his rice and oil mills at Prangin Road. Rice merchants from Rangoon had invested in Phuah Hin Leong's earlier milling enterprise.

In the early 20th century, managed by

HUTTENBACH GODOWNS

In Penang, household electricity supply was introduced by August Huttenbach. The German first came to Penang in 1872 as an assistant to Katz Brothers. He and his brother Ludwig then founded the firm Huttenbach Brothers, Penang and Singapore.

The company ran the first regular ships to Aceh, and started the first steamship services to the Coromandel Coast to bring Indian labour into the country. Huttenbach's ships carried European mail from India without charge as a service to Penang.

The business then diversified into ice works and the manufacture of building materials, including the decorative floor tiles so commonly found in Penang's prewar houses. Huttenbach also lit up the streets of Penang and Taiping (see also Beach Street). Keeping up with the latest mechanical and electrical technology, the company then introduced the first electricity plants to Penang.

Although he ran a large concern in

Above, Khie Heng Bee Mills - these and Huttenbach's Godowns are actually located on the north side of the Pinang River on the former Bridge Street, but mark the beginning of the Jelutong industrial area.

Singapore, the German chose to live in Penang and work for its improvement through private initiative. Huttenbach became a naturalised British subject and then a Legislative Councillor in the 1890s.

SYED SHEIKH AL-HADI'S RESIDENCE

As a young man, Syed Sheikh Al-Hadi's friendship with the Riau royalty allowed him to travel to Egypt, where he was influenced by a leading Islamic reformist.

After returning to the Straits Settlements, he co-founded several Jawi magazines *Al-Imam* (1906), *Al-Ikhwan* and *Saudara;* the last two were printed at his Jelutong Press in the 1920s.

In 1926, he authored *Hikayat Faridah Hanom*, based on an Egyptian novel. It was the first novel written in the Malay vernacular, and became a best-seller among the Malay public. Like his other publications, "The Story of Faridah Hanom" expressed his modernist views of Islam.

In 1919, Al-Hadi became the headmaster of *Madrasatul Mashoor Al-Islamiyah.* The school, founded by several Arabs, was started in Acheen Street in 1916 and moved to Kampung Jawa Lama in 1917, and eventually to Tek Soon Street. It became the leading centre for Islamic and Arab education in Southeast Asia.

Al-Hadi's house has since been bought over by vegetarian nuns who use it as a temple. On the first and fifteenth of each month, vegetarian meals are served to the public.

MESJID MAQBUL

In the early years, the Pinang River was used by Acehnese and Malay traders as the link to the interior of the island. Mesjid Maqbul started out as a shelter and prayer hall *(surau)* built with *nibong* palm. It was rebuilt in brick in 1850, and known then as *Mesjid Tuan Guru* (see also Acheen Street).

The congregation was split after the Penang Riots of 1867, and a section went off to found the adjacent *Mesjid Bahru* (New Mosque); thenceforth, Mesjid Maqbul came to be referred to as *Mesjid Lama Sungai Pinang* (Sungai Pinang Old Mosque).

Above, Sheikh Al-Hadi's former Malay-Palladian residence. Below, the Mesjid Maqbul.

on the east coast of South India, the Mericans were sea-borne traders - *Marakayar* being the Arabic word for "ship" or "guidance of Allah" (see also Noordin Family Tomb, Chulia Street).

Among the Muslim traders, it was the Mericans who controlled the shipping business in Penang in the first century, playing a similar role to certain Arab families in Singapore.

The Tamil Muslims, in particular the Merican, Sahib and Lebai clans, were probably the most powerful group of Indian merchants trading in the Straits of Malacca during Francis Light's time.

Cauder Merican led a community of Tamil Muslim traders from the Kedah coast to come and settle in Penang. Light appointed him Kapitan Kling, head of the Indian community. *Keling* is the term applied by the locals to South Indians, just as *Bengali* is their generic term for North Indians.

In 1801, a grant for the 18-acre site was given to Kapitan Kling as founder of the mosque; the land was described as bounded towards the west and south by lands privately owned by Kapitan Kling. When he died in 1834, the whole of Kapitan Kling's property amounted to an astounding 50,000 Spanish Dollars.

The man himself lived at Kampong Kolam (Pool Village) - so called because of a large granite tank in the compound of Kapitan Kling's house, in front of the present tomb.

Kapitan Kling is buried in the covered

KAMPONG DELI

The port of Medan, Deli, in North Sumatra is situated directly across the Straits of Malacca from Penang.

The Sumatran community who lived at Kampong Deli reared the sturdy Acehnese ponies which were especially useful to transport passengers and goods up Penang Hill.

Many old stables and mews survive in George Town - those near Kampong Deli at Ariffin Court are used as a taxi stand, while others have been converted into living quarters or motor showrooms.

KAMPONG KOLAM

KAPITAN KLING'S TOMB

The first permanent mosque on the island was founded by Kapitan Kling alias Cauder Mydin Merican (see also Kapitan Kling Mosque, Pitt Street).

Hailing from Tanjore district, Tamil Nadu,

A house in Kampong Deli.

tomb built by Indian masons, together with his three wives. His first wife was Pattani Amah Othman Nachiar, who is regarded as a saint or *keramat*. His second wife was Tunku Maheran alias Tunku Wanchik Thaibu, a princess from the Kedah royal house and his third wife, a Malay woman named Che Aminah.

Rents from the surrounding private charity lands were to go towards upkeeping the mausoleum, organising feasts *(kenduri)* and maintaining the tank *(tangki)* for the use of the poor. A road was made through Kampong Kolam at the turn of the century, cutting off the Armenian Street houses at their backs (see also Pitt Street).

The adjacent Kampong Kaka was named after a Malabari family which lived on the west side of Kampong Kolam (see also Kampong Malabar). *Kaka* and *Mamak* are polite addresses for Malabar Muslims and Tamil Muslims respectively.

KAMPONG MALABAR

The Malabaris, who speak Malayalam, hail from Kerala on the west coast of South India. As early convict labourers, the Malabaris were reputed to have built most of the government buildings in Penang.

Among them were also craftsmen who were responsible for the masonry and fine plasterwork found in Penang's elite Muslim homes and prestigious civic buildings.

Even after Penang ceased to be a penal station, Malabari construction workers continued to be employed by Chinese and Indian contractors as well as the Public Works

Department until as late as the 1930s, when they built the Police Headquarters at Dickens Street (see also Penang Road).

Some ex-convicts became petty traders and were the core group who started the Chowrasta Market.

Kampong Malabar was taken over by Japanese and Chinese shops at the turn of the century. Today it is a popular hawker food area by night.

KATZ STREET

The Katz Bros, Ltd. were established in 1864 by Hermann Katz (a naturalised Englishman) and his brother. When the Dutch were at war with Aceh in the 1870s, the Katz Brothers secured the contract to ship all supplies to the Dutch army for three years. They chartered vessels from Khoo Tiang Poh for the purpose.

As local traders were embargoed from the Acehnese pepper ports, the Katz Brothers managed to corner the supply of pepper within a few years. The Singapore-based company thus prospered and opened branches in Penang and Sumatra, as well as in London and Frankfurt.

Kapitan Kling's Tomb.

KEDAH ROAD

Among the famous personalities from Kedah Road were Abdullah Ariff (d. 1962), a Municipal Councillor and one of Penang's pioneer modern painters.

In spite of its official road name, Kedah Road was really *Kampong Melaka,* as testified by the local names in both Malay and Chinese. The families here made and sold *cincaluk* and other Malaccan specialities.

Kedah Road is a former Peranakan Jawi neighbourhood with some fine surviving examples of early domestic architecture.

Already in the first half of the 19th century, the Anglo-Indian masonry bungalow had combined with the traditional Malay timber house to produce the half-masonry, half-timber Indo-Malay house of the *Jawi Peranakan* community. Some common elements subsequently influenced traditional Malay house design.

In contrast to the Georgian symmetry of the Anglo-Indian house, the homes of the Peranakan Jawi community are marked by a strong Malay asymmetry, with an *anjung* or porch set off to one side. Covered stairs lead up to the hall on the first floor.

The Indo-Malay houses typically have a masonry ground floor and a timber upper floor with full-length louvred windows for open ventilation, sometimes incorporating Indian dentilation and Georgian fanlights.

A special feature of the examples found in the Kedah Road neighbourhood are the tiled "Malacca stairs". The semi-hipped roofs found here are similar to those of the Chulia Street bungalows (see also Chulia Street).

Similar Indo-Malay houses can be also found along Transfer Road, Hutton Lane, Burmah Road and Penang Road. Survivors of former villages, most of these early bungalows are set back from the main roads and some are concealed by street-fronting shophouses of later vintage.

HIDAYATHUL MUSLIM ASSOCIATION

Today, the residents of Kedah Road are mostly Tamil Muslims from the village of Kadaiyanallur in India (see also United Muslim Association, Transfer Road). Some belong to the Hidayathul Muslim Association which was formed in the 1940s.

The first president, Haji S. O. Mohd. Mohideen was a spice merchant who supplied his *giling rempah* and curries to the leading *nasi kandar* restaurants in Penang.

The Hidayathul Muslim Association in an Indo-Malay house with Malacca stairs and fine dentilation.

KELAWAI ROAD

The word comes from *Kuala Awal* meaning "the first estuary" - presumably the first river west of George Town. This area was cleared by Malays. Two old mosques, the Mesjid Lama and the Mesjid Kelawei, were founded in the early 1800s and rebuilt at the turn of the century.

The western end of Kelawai Road was largely an Eurasian Catholic area. The Catholic cemetery was reserved for Eurasians until as late as the 1970s (see also Church of Immaculate Conception, Burmah Road and College Square). Across the road are still some characteristic Eurasian homes.

The St. Joseph's Novitiate building of 1916 is being used by the Uplands School, which caters mainly to expatriate children. Next to it is the former site of the College-General (see also College Square).

JIMMY BOYLE'S HOUSE

The most famous son of the Penang Eurasian community was the outstanding Malaysian composer and jazz musician, Jimmy Boyle (d.1971).

He resided at Kelawai Road in the 1950s and 60s, during some of his most prolific years (see also Church of Immaculate Conception, Burmah Road).

KIMBERLEY STREET

The Earl of Kimberley was Secretary of State for the Colonies in the 1870s.

The eastern end of Kimberley Street used to be an extension of the Acheen Street neighbourhood; a small side lane named Lorong Ngah Aboo recalls the former Acehnese community here.

Kimberley Street is locally called *Sua Thau Kay* - Swatow being a port in Teochew district in the Kwangtung province of China. It was also called *Mee Sua Kay* or "Vermicelli Street", as the Teochews made rice noodles and dried them by the roadside.

The neighbourhood is still predominantly Teochew, with a deep-rooted "Chinatown" character. Here you find shops selling joss sticks and Teochew food. The hawker stalls at Kimberley Street are well-patronised by locals at suppertime.

Jimmy Boyle's house built in the late 1920s. Below, Kimberley Street with its Chinatown character.

KING STREET

Southern Indian Muslim sailors and stevedores lived along certain parts of King Street, which the Tamils call *Padavukara Tharuva* or "The Street of Boatmen".

As one of the earliest main streets, it has no less than a dozen Chinese association buildings and temples, reflecting the activities of the Hakka, Hokkien, Cantonese and Sing Ling dialect groups.

CHONG SAN WOOI KOON

An association of the Cantonese dialect group, founded in the early 1800s, built in the mid-19th century. Dr. Sun Yat Sen alias Sun Chong San hailed from Heong San district, Kwangtung province. The district was renamed Chong San in his honour, and the association changed its name accordingly.

TUA PEK KONG TEMPLE

This section of King Street is called *Kuin-Tang Tua-Pek-Kong Kay* (Cantonese Tua Pek Kong Street), as the Tua Pek Kong Temple here is controlled by the Cantonese and Hakka dialect groups - in contrast to the Hokkien Tua Pek Kong Temple at Armenian Street. This temple is a branch of the Tua Pek Kong Temple in Tanjong Tokong (see also Tanjong Tokong).

TOI SAN NIN YONG HUI KWON & WU TI MEOW

An association of the Sing Ling dialect group, Toi San district, Kwangtung province. The Wu Ti Meow (War Emperor's Temple) is the temple component of the Toi

KING EDWARD PLACE

VICTORIA MEMORIAL CLOCKTOWER

To commemorate Queen Victoria's Diamond Jubilee, Cheah Chen Eok donated this 60-foot high clocktower - one foot for each year of Her Majesty's reign in 1897. The Queen had died by the time the clocktower was finally completed in 1902.

The leaning clocktower of George Town acquired its tilt when bombs were dropped on King Edward Place during the last war, destroying the Government Buildings.

The monument has given rise to fond tales - if you listened closely, you would hear it say, *Tick-tock, tick-tock, I am Chen Eok, I gave this clock, tick-tock, tick-tock...*

The Queen Victoria Memorial Clocktower

San association. It is dedicated to Kwan Kong, a war general in the epic of the *Three Kingdoms,* who represents strength, chivalry and honour.

He is the patron deity of the Toi San people, and an important deity for the Cantonese people in general. Cantonese businessmen call upon the Kwan Kong to witness their spoken agreements.

The signboard over the temple entrance was written by Leong Ting Fen, a central government officer in China who worked as a teacher and calligrapher while in exile in the 1890s for criticizing the Prime Minister. After the Boxer Rebellion, he regained imperial favour - the Empress Dowager appointed him tutor of Pu Yi, the last emperor of China.

Both temple and association building acquired

their Cantonese-style structures in the 1890s. The prominent profiles are styled after traditional "horse head" gables.

NG SEE KAH MEOW

The Ng surname clan association was renovated to its present form around 1913. The front hall is decorated with Art Nouveau tiles and traditional Chinese flower stands. An early 19th century house was incorporated and concealed at the back.

Above, an ensemble of five associations and temples at the junction of Church and King Streets. Below, Wu Ti Meow at left, and the Ng See Kah Meow at right.

TSENG LUNG FUI KON

An association of the Hakka dialect group from Tseng Lung district, Kwangtung province, founded in 1802. The mid-19th century premises were renovated in 1922.

KAR YIN FOOI KOON

An association of the Hakka dialect group from Kar Yin district, Kwangtung province, founded in 1801. Low Amee was one of the founders (see also Ayer Itam). The mid-19th century premises were rebuilt around 1940.

LEE SIH CHONG SOO

The Lee surname clan association, housed in a Straits Eclectic style shophouse temple, was founded in the 1920s.

Membership was originally restricted to members of a specific Lee clan from the Tang Ua district, Hokkien province who were mainly based in a clan jetty at Weld Quay.

Clan members regard themselves as descended from the founder of the Tang dynasty and trace their ancestry ultimately to the philosopher Lao Tzu.

A large portrait of Dr. Sun Yat Sen still hangs in their front hall.

KU CHEN HOOI

The "Old Castle Meeting" is a 19th century association dedicated to the sworn brothers of the Three Kingdoms - Lu Pei, Chang Fei, and Kwan Kong.

Members are those bearing any one of these three surnames.

Above left, the Tseng Lung Fui Koon, next to another Hakka association the Kar Yin Fooi Koon. Above right, the Lee Sih Chong Soo - the centre unit of three shophouses was renovated into a temple in the 1920s.

POE CHOO SEAH

A 19th century association of the "Straits-born Chinese", reconstituted in 1893 with Cheah Chen Eok as the Chairman (see also Victoria Memorial Clocktower). The building was completed in 1903.

FORMER HO SENG SOCIETY BASE

Unfortunately, this mid-19th century building has been extensively modernized and only the old fanlights indicate its antiquity.

The section between China Street and Market Street was formerly called "Old Ho Seng Secret Society Street".

CHIN SI TONG SOO

The Chin surname clan association, Sing Ling dialect, Toi San district, Kwangtung province, founded in 1876. The premises were rebuilt in the 1910s in Cantonese Eclectic style.

The building has a triple-storey section at the back with striking "fire gables".

Above, the three-storey Poe Choo Seah and the former Ho Seng Society Base. Middle, the Chin Si Tong Soo. Below, the Tua Pek Kong Temple - temple architecture adapted to shophouse context.

two Anglo-Chinese schools, subsequently named Methodist Boys' School and Methodist Girls' Schools.

LARUT ROAD

LIMBURG

The mansion which houses the Kentucky Fried Chicken restaurant was named "Limburg" - however not after the German town which produces the pungent cheese.

It was rather the private haven of Lim Cheng Teik, eldest son of the miller Phuah Hin Leong (see also Phuah Hin Leong Road).

At 26, Lim Cheng Teik became the youngest Municipal Commissioner in the history of Penang. *Limburg* was drawn up in 1917 by Neubronner's firm.

The adaptive reuse of Limburg was designed by the American architects of the Kentucky Fried Chicken Corporation.

THE WESLEY METHODIST CHURCH

The Church was founded in 1891 by American missionaries, shortly after they started their mission in Singapore. It was built around 1911 as the FitzGerald Memorial Church, in memory of a visiting Bishop and his daughter who died in 1907.

The Methodist mission was responsible for establishing three major schools within a short time - the Pykett Methodist School and

LEITH STREET

During George Leith's term as Lieutenant-Governor of Penang (1800-1803), Province Wellesley was secured, the pepper trade was boosted and a 300-ton teak frigate called "Penang" was built for the East India Company's service.

Leith reorganised the local government, fixed assessments, supervised the public works carried out by convict labour and set up a regular administration of justice, of which he himself took the role of Judge and Magistrate.

Above left, Limburg. Above right, Wesley Methodist Church. Below, Cathay Hotel, a budget heritage hotel, formerly Yeoh Wee Gark's mansion.

The Leith administration was the first to issue proper land grants, and that is why most early institutions, though they may already have existed in Light's time, can only date their founding to the early 1800s.

Leith Street used to be lined with palm trees and thus the Malay name for it is *Nyior Cabang*.

At the turn of the century, Leith Street was "Hakka Millionaire's Row". Cheong Fatt Tze was foremost among the Hakka towkays who lived down the street - these included

Cheah Choon Seng, Cheah's in-law Leong Fee, and Tye Kee Yoon. When Cheong Fatt Tze was promoted to serve as Consul-General in Singapore, his neighbours took turns to play Vice-Consul of China in Penang.

Cheong Fatt Tze, his cousin Chang Yu Nan who was Mayor of Deli, and Cheah Choon Seng who was Kapitan China of Aceh, moved to Penang in the late 19th century. They joined forces with Penang's leading Hakkas such as Chung Keng Kwee, and invested their capital in the tin-mines of Perak (see also Chung Keng Kwee Temple, Church Street).

The Hakka tycoons of Leith Street were partners in business, as well as joint benefactors educational institutions and charities. Cheong Fatt Tze, Chang Yu Nan, Cheah Choon Seng, Tye Kee Yoon and Chung Keng Kwee were the Five Great Sponsors to Kek Lok Si; their miniature statues are preserved there.

Above, Konsenih building, formerly the mansion of Leong Fee, father of Leong Yin Kean (see Northam Road). Below, Leith Street Pub, formerly Tye Kee Yoon's home, designed by Chew Eng Eam.

CHEONG FATT TZE MANSION

Cheong Fatt Tze alias Chang Pi Shih alias Thio Tiauw Siat was a powerful Nanyang industrialist and a first-class Mandarin in the service of the Manchu government. In the 1890s, he was director of China's railway works and its first modern banking institution.

As a special trade commissioner, he raised vast funds from the Chinese in Southeast Asia to industrialize and modernize China.

Under the Republican Government, Yuan Shi-Kai sent him to seek investments from the Chinese industralists in America. The New York Times reported his visit, dubbing him "China's Rockefeller".

Due to political circumstances, his contributions towards the Chinese government's efforts did not bear fruit. In contrast, his own corporation, the Chang Yue Pioneer Wine Company in Teochew district was highly

successful and even survived nationalization under the Communist government. It was the first agricultural enterprise in China run with Western management and employing a scientific approach.

Cheong Fatt Tze (1840-1917) a Hakka from Tai Pu in Teochew district, migrated to Java to seek his fortune in the 1850s. He prospered rapidly and expanded his business to Sumatra, operating steamships between Medan, North Sumatra and Penang.

As one of the leading Nanyang Chinese, he was offered the post of Vice-Consul of China. The Dutch East Indies did not allow diplomatic representation, so he moved his base to Penang in the early 1890s.

A few years later, he was promoted to Consul-General in Singapore, and continued building an empire of trading, shipping, opium, agriculture and mining in Southeast Asia. At the height of his career, he became

The Cheong Fatt Tze Mansion was used as a location for the French film "Indo-Chine" in 1991.

economic advisor to the Empress Dowager.

He saw education as the means to bring the Chinese into the 20th century, hence he played the main benefactor of the Chung Hwa Confucian School in Penang, the first modern Chinese school in the country. He also helped to found the Eng Sin School in Singapore and the Western programme at Hong Kong university.

Cheong Fatt Tze's fabulous courtyard mansion was built over seven years (1896-1904). Plans for further expansion, including the construction of bathrooms, were left unexecuted. Cheong Fatt Tze had eight wives and owned lavish residences throughout his trading empire. However, the Penang mansion was his principal home, where he raised his six sons, whom he sent for western education at the St. Xavier's Institution.

Though it resembles a courtyard mansion in layout, the Cheong Fatt Tze Mansion with its seven staircases incorporated western decorations such as stained glass, fake wood veneer and decorative ceiling mouldings. The central courtyard balcony combined Victorian cast iron with Chinese lattice work.

The Chinese gilded woodcarved doors and panels, ceramic shard decorations on the roofs, gables and walls, as well as the intricate ceramic shard tableaux on the first floor verandah, are of the highest quality.

Cheong Fatt Tze's east-facing mansion is approached through a Chinese gate, and exited through a western-style gate. It reflects his life-long mission to introduce modern reforms to China. An old picture shows him dressed in suit and top hat, and another in mandarin attire; these were the two faces of Cheong Fatt Tze, and other Nanyang Chinese of his time, who tried to combine the best of East and West to bring progress to the worldwide Chinese community.

Above left, the courtyard used as a film set. Above right, the stained glass windows. Below, the ceramic shard decorations at the front balcony.

LEITH STREET GHAUT

This street was formerly called "Martina's Lane" after the Portuguese Eurasian Martina Rozells, without whom Francis Light may never have founded Penang.

Francis Light lived with Martina in a bungalow on the site of the St. Xavier's field, and Martina continued to stay there after she was remarried to John Timmers.

A chapter of Francis Light's will reads:

I give and bequeath unto the said Martina Rozells my Bungaloe in George Town with the Ground thereunto belonging with one set of Mahogany Tables, two Card Tables, Two Couches, two Bedstead large and two small with Bedding ... a dressing table and 18 chairs, two Silver Candlesticks, one Silver Teapot two sugar dishes, twelve table spoons, twelve tea spoons, one soup spoon (Silver) and all the utensils not under the Stewards charge to be by her disposed of as she thinks proper without any limitation. I give also unto the said Martina Rozells four of my best Cows and one Bull...

On the west side of the lane are some fine government quarters along the casuarina lined beach. This was the site of *Mount Airy,* which Light gave to Captain Francis Simpson on the condition that it would not be disposed to anyone "whom the said Francis Light may deem unpleasant neighbours to himself".

Government quarters at Leith Street Ghaut today (demolished)

LIGHT STREET

Captain Francis Light, as the first Superintendent of the Prince of Wales Island, named the settlement's first street after himself (see also Francis Light Memorial, Farquhar Street).

As his "first municipal act", Light sank a public well at the end of Light Street - the one-acre Well Estate is now part of the Convent Grounds. Light himself lived to the west of the Well Estate, on the site which is now the St. Xavier's field (Leith Street Ghaut).

All the early government buildings and European residences were lined up along Light Street, hugging the North Beach. The Fort, the Municipal Council Buildings and the State Assembly Hall around the Esplanade comprised the nucleus of a large civic park which extended to Downing Street and Farquhar Street.

FORT CORNWALLIS

Soon after taking possession of the island, Francis Light erected a fort of *nibong* palm at the landing point at the tip of the cape. With the first batch of convict labour despatched from India, Light had the fort rebuilt in brick at the cost of 67,000 Spanish Dollars, without waiting for approval from his superiors in Bengal.

The Fort Cornwallis, named after the Governor-General of Bengal, was by no means adequate. Colonel Wellesley, who was later to become the Duke of Wellington, remarked in 1797 that, "As the town and fort stand now, it is impossible to defend them".

Governor Farquhar in 1804-5 repaired the fort and built a new half-moon battery at

a further 71,000 Spanish Dollars - an outrageous sum, especially since the battery, instead of contributing to the fortifications, fell into the sea soon afterward.

When Penang was elevated to a Presidency in 1805, there were plans to rebuild a fort further inland, but that would have meant demolishing the existing fort and half the commercial town!

Various plans for a new fort were deemed too costly, and so the existing one was substantially rebuilt around 1810, during Norman Macalister's term as Governor.

In the East India Company's maps and early correspondence, Penang was sometimes referred to as *Fort Cornwallis*. However, the fort has historically been used for administration rather than defence.

Early pictures show the star-shaped fort crowded with buildings for the military offices and barracks. Among the few structures which survive are a gunpowder magazine and a chapel for Christian worship. The fort was surrounded by a moat, which has since been filled in.

The first recorded service which took place in the fort's chapel was the marriage of Francis Light's widow, Martina Rozells, to John Timmers in 1799.

At the northeastern point are the flagstaff and harbour light to signal incoming ships. The flagstaff also communicated with another at Bel Retiro on Penang Hill - hence the latter's official name "Flagstaff Hill" - announcing the arrival of mailships or important visitors which might occasion the Governor's descent from his comfortable hill abode.

Today, the Fort Cornwallis is managed as a cultural venue and a small admission fee is charged. An amphitheatre built in recent decades is used for performances.

Fort Cornwallis, shaped like a four-pointed star. The flagstaff is posted at the northeastern point, the gunpowder magazine can still be seen at the northwestern point of the star and the chapel at the southwestern point.

SERI RAMBAI

This legendary demi-cannon bears the cipher of the Dutch East India Company, as well as heraldic lions and dolphins.

The Dutch gave it to the Sultan of Johore around the year 1605, in the prospect of being allowed to erect a fort there.

In 1613, Batu Sawar, then the capital of Johore, was sacked by Mahkota Alam, the Sultan of Aceh, who captured the cannon along with the Johore royal family. This event is inscribed on the cannon in Jawi calligraphy inlaid in silver wire.

In 1795, the Sultan of Aceh gave it to the Sultan of Selangor for his cooperation in a war. It defended the fort there until 1871 when Kuala Selangor was seized by the Madras Native Infantry in retribution for an attack on Penang.

Despite or perhaps because of its violent past, the cannon is a potent symbol to local women who place flowers on the barrel to enhance their fertility.

FOO TYE SIN'S MANSION

Light Street and the North Beach was the preserve of the European elite until the mid-19th century, when a few members of the non-European community proved so wealthy and refined that they could no longer be excluded.

Among the first non-Europeans to erect their mansions along Light Street were two business partners, Koh Seang Tat and Foo Tye Sin (after whom Tye Sin Street is named).

Foo Tye Sin's mansion (now the MUI Bank building) dates from the mid-19th century. It has a four-storey lookout tower at the back, and used to be guarded by a Chinese gate and wall.

KOH SEANG TAT'S FOUNTAIN

Koh Seang Tat donated a fountain to the Town Hall when the latter opened in 1883. He was the grandson of Koh Lay Huan (see also China Street) and the first Chinese to be appointed Justice of the Peace.

In 1887, Seang Tat, Cheah Chen Eok (who was Foo Tye Sin's son-in-law) and Dr. W.C. Brown were the first elected members of the Municipal Commission.

Above, Seri Rambai, the potent cannon. Below, Foo Tye Sin's mansion.

Unlike so many of the fanciful names given to elite residences, Koh Seang Tat's *Edinburgh Castle* was truly earned. When the Duke of Edinburgh visited Penang in 1869, the Municipal Commissioners were hard pressed to provide suitable premises. Seang Tat came to the rescue by offering his mansion on Light Street, then the grandest in town, with comforts befitting the Duke.

The road which led to the *Edinburgh House* was afterward named Duke Road. The *Dewan Sri Pinang,* a public multi-purpose hall designed by the Public Works Department, now stands on the site.

Seang Tat also built a similar abode in Balik Pulau, where his family owned large estates. The fountain which he donated to Balik Pulau town still stands in the middle of the main street.

THE STATE ASSEMBLY BUILDINGS

These Anglo-Indian classical-style public buildings date from the early 19th century. They served as Recorder's Courts and Magistrate's Courts, forming part of what was formerly the Central Police Station.

The Chinese called Light Street *Po Le Khau* which meant "the entrance to the Police Courts".

The buildings, which face the Esplanade, were renovated in 1874. In 1890, an administrative block (now the Immigration Building) was added.

Today, they house the chambers of the State Assembly. A fleet of Mercedes Benzes parked out in front usually means that State Assembly is in session.

Above, State Assembly Buildings. Below, Detail of Koh Seang Tat's fountain.

THE CONVENT LIGHT STREET

The Convent is the oldest girls' school in the country and one of the few inner city schools left in George Town. It occupies a remarkable complex of buildings constructed over a span of almost two centuries.

Three French Sisters of the Holy Infant Jesus Mission arrived in Penang in 1852 to work among the poor and start a school for girls. They were joined in the same year by Mother St. Mathilde, considered the main founder of the Mission in Malaya which grew to over 80 convent schools. She also founded the mission in Japan in 1872.

In 1859, the Mission acquired a seven-acre site at the end of Light Street, with the Government House on it. The Convent expanded with an Old Chapel (1867), the Old Hall, cloisters and classrooms (1882), and new extensions in 1901, 1929 and 1934.

Part of the original classroom complex was adapted to house the New Chapel, consecrated in 1932, with an early Art Deco style interior.

The Convent, located in the middle of town yet isolated from the outside world, is steeped in human history. It contained a nunnery, a novitiate, a chapel, an orphanage for the town's unwanted ba-

Above, the abandoned classrooms. Below, the interior - the upper floor consists of a long colonnaded gallery.

bies and a boarding school. The Malays called the Convent *arpang,* referring to the orphanage.

Fees from the "first-class" boarders, who were the daughters of distant elite families, subsidized the poor "second-class" boarders. Malay was the common language between the French sisters, the boarders and the orphans.

The Convent Light Street was a premier girls' school which drew students from all over the country, and as far as Thailand and Indonesia. A former student was Miss Apasara, Thailand's first Miss Universe, who took up secretarial courses in the 1960's at the commercial school (in the old Government House).

During the Second World War, the Convent was occupied by the Japanese Navy who took American prisoners from the USS Grenadier SS 210 in 1943. The naval officers were incarcerated in "Block C" and tortured in the Art Room.

Their names, scratched on the wall with the tip of a belt buckle, are preserved behind glass. Many of the prisoners returned to visit the Convent after the war, and one of them, Albert Rupp, wrote a book entitled "Threshold of Hell" about his experience.

The original French stained glass windows in the Chapel were shattered by Japanese bombs. They were later replaced by the same workshop in France.

Above, the Old Hall. Below left, the stained glass windows of the Convent Chapel. Below right, the "C" Block, where the American POWs were detained.

THE GOVERNMENT HOUSE

The Government House was acquired by the Convent in 1859 and still stands in the school grounds today. In the early years of the Convent, it served as a Novitiate.

The Government House built by Farquhar in 1804 survives in highly original condition. This early Anglo-Indian style public building, probably the most important example in the country, is not yet gazetted.

The Government House stands on Light's former town property, right next to the "Well Estate". After Light's death, the land passed to his trading partner, James Scott, who leased it to the East India Company government. The latter paid a rent of 250 Spanish Dollars a month in 1805, besides having to keep the house and sea wall in good repair.

The Government House was the first non-military seat of the East India Company government in Penang, housing the Governor's Office and Council Chambers.

The building was completed before

Farquhar left, just in time for the incoming Presidency government. Governor Phillip Dundas arrived with an expanded staff, among whom was the young Stamford Raffles as Assistant Secretary.

The industrious and ambitious Raffles must have spent much time here, as he was

Top, the Government House in the Convent. Bottom, the southern entrance hall.

wont to take on the responsibilities of his ill, fatigued, uninspired or expired colleagues, besides creating new ones for himself.

The most distinguished visitor to the Government House was the Governor-General of India Lord Minto. In 1811, stopping by enroute to Java, he addressed the Penang Government in the Council Chamber, temporarily "converting this small Presidency into the Supreme Government of India".

Tunku Syed Hussain came to pay his respects to Lord Minto, just before the Governor-General departed from the Government House. The party proceeded along a covered walkway and straight out to a boat docked along the North Beach.

From here, Lord Minto went on to Malacca, where Munshi Abdullah witnessed his meeting with Raffles. The two of them then embarked on the famous Java Expedition.

The Government House was built by convicts, at a time when a hundred of them were employed in the Company's kilns to make bricks and plaster. The walls were originally covered with Madras *chunam,* a type of plaster made from egg shell or oyster-shell, which gave the appearance of white marble when polished. The stucco details, depicting birds and cannons, are uniquely evocative of the East India Company days.

Above right and left, stucco details. Below, the eastern staircase.

SUPREME COURT BUILDING

The court house has been sited here since 1809. The present Supreme Court Building was constructed in 1905 at a cost of 206,678 Straits Dollars.

The Public Library used to occupy the wing facing the St. George's Church, before it was relocated to the Dewan Sri Pinang.

LOGAN MEMORIAL

In the grounds of the Supreme Court is a memorial to James Richardson Logan, a man who devoted his life to justice and knowledge. On the marble slab is inscribed, "He was an erudite and skillful lawyer, an eminent scientific ethnologist and he has founded a literature for these settlements..."

James Richardson Logan and his elder brother Abraham studied law in Edinburgh. At Duns Academy, James was a classmate of

David Brown's son, Forbes Scott Brown, who was later to assist him in his Penang career.

The Logan brothers came to the Straits Settlements around 1840, after a brief stint as indigo planters in India.

In Penang, James rose to prominence by defending an Indian *sireh* planter's appeal against the East India Company.

He skilfully expounded the case in the press, bringing it before the tribunal of public opinion, and was finally admitted to the Penang bar as a law agent to represent the planter.

Around 1842, the Logan brothers went to practise in Singapore. Abraham became editor of the *Singapore Free Press* from 1846 until several years before his retirement to Penang in 1868.

The next year James founded the *Journal of the Indian Archipelago and Eastern Asia* in 27 volumes, also called *Logan's Journals,*

James was known as the champion of the non-European communities. When the police attempted to suppress all potential secret society activities, James as legal advisor to the Chinese merchants submitted petitions on their behalf, which resulted in official recognition being given to certain organisations and festivals.

Owning plantations in Province Wellesley, James voiced his concern about the environment in an article entitled, *The Probable Effects On The Climate Of Pinang Of The Continued Destruction Of Its Hill Jungles*, published in his journal in 1848.

His death from malaria on 20th October 1869 was regarded as a "public calamity" and a memorial was erected to him by the people of the Straits Settlements. A short account of his life was written by his close friend, the government surveyor and artist John Turnbull Thomson.

Logan Road was named after him.

of which he was writer, editor and publisher from 1847 to 1859.

His *Language and Ethnology of the Indian Archipelago* promoted an understanding of the peoples and cultures of the Nusantara region.

The younger brother returned to practise in Penang in 1853, working in partnership with his brother Abraham in Singapore. James also took over a newspaper, the *Pinang Gazette,* and was apparently responsible for persuading the P & O Liners to call at Penang.

Through the press, the Logan brothers widely influenced public opinion in the Straits Settlements and encouraged the agitation for an end to Indian rule, which resulted in the Transfer of 1867 (see also Transfer Road.)

Above, Logan Memorial. Below, the western side of the memorial, showing Logan's profile.

LOVE LANE

Love Lane is full of intimate places such as the Wan Hai Hotel, the sound of which has lusty connotations, boasting the narrowest five-foot way in town. Here are a coffeeshop, down the road from the Carpenter's Guild, where construction workers congregate, and *Lim Tan Tin,* a workshop which carves Mah Jung tiles and Chinese dice.

Formerly inhabited by Eurasians who lived around the church at Farquhar Street, the Chinese who moved into Love Lane after them called it *Serani Hung,* or "Eurasian Lane".

There are many theories about the origin of the name "Love Lane". Some say this

was where the sailors met the island's ladies among the bamboo groves. The local Chinese say the rich men who lived on Muntri Street kept their mistresses here, hence the name *Ai Cheng Hang.*

But one story is so extraordinary that it probably has some basis in reality.

Love Lane already appears in a map of 1803. The following story must belong to the earliest chapter of Penang's history, when there were many Shia Muslims among both the North Indian sepoys and convicts.

During the Muharram festival in Penang, the Shia Muslims staged processions to commemorate the violent death of Ali, the son-in-law of the Prophet Muhammad, and Ali's two sons Hassan and Hussain.

Above, Love Lane. Below, the Sun Tak Association

The Shiite devotees performed pain-defying rituals with swords, skewers and coals, much like those seen in the Hindu Thaipusam procession or the Chinese Nine Emperor Gods festival. Even more extreme forms of self-torture found in these festivals, such as swinging from tenterhooks, have since been banned.

The procession, which featured representations of the martyrs' tombs made of paper and tinsel, toured the Indian Muslim areas in town. It gathered the largest crowd along Chulia Street, before proceeding through Love Lane toward the north beach. There, the tabuts would be cast into the sea, and the devotees would take part in ritual bathing known as *mandi safar*.

Onlookers could not help but be awed by this spectacle of self-flagellation, which intensified as the devotees approached the end of their procession. With each painful step they shouted the names of the martyrs, "Hassan! Hussain!"

To conclude, Love Lane was given its name to remember the impressive feats of suffering undertaken here *for the love of Hussain*.

SUN TAK ASSOCIATION

This Cantonese district association was founded in 1838. Its present premises were refurbished in 1928.

From Sun Tak district came a large number of male butchers and female domestic servants called *mah cheh*. The *mah cheh* who wore their long hair in pigtails are a subgroup of the Cantonese *amah*, who generally have their hair up in a bun as a sign of being married to the sisterhood (see also Muntri Street).

CARPENTER'S GUILD

Carpentry is the first of all Chinese building trades and Lo Pan is the patron saint of all building practitioners, from craftsmen and contractors to engineers and architects. The Lo Pan Hang was once considered the mother temple of all Chinese building guilds in the country.

Carpenters and brick-layers were among the first Cantonese tradesmen to settle in Penang. In 1794, Francis Light wrote that, "The Chinese residents are the most skilfull carpenters, construction workers and machinery workers." Most of the original carpenters and goldsmiths were Cantonese of the Sing Ling dialect group.

During the 19th century, every Chinese craftsman and builder who came to Malaysia would first call at the Lo Pan temple in Penang before proceeding to the other states to work. While some craftsmen settled in the country, there were also many who were brought from China on short-term contracts to work on the magnificent temples and mansions all over the country.

The Lo Pan Hang was founded in 1850 in a shophouse at 5 Penang Street (still extant). In 1865, a proper temple called the *Lo Pan Ku Miou,* or "North Duke Old Castle" was built as a free-standing building on Love Lane.

Lo Pan is a historical figure, a contemporary of Confucius and Mencius and China's equivalent of Leonardo da Vinci. He is attributed with the invention of many of the basic tools used by carpenters today.

According to the legend, he retreated to the mountains at the age of 27 and there invented the collapsible umbrella, the saw and axe, the extendable ladder and string puppet mechanism. Like Da Vinci, he also

Under the medieval guild system, the crafts were passed down from master to apprentice. An apprenticeship lasted for three years, during which time the novice was provided only food and board.

The guild comprised masters and apprentices, who formed the West Wing, and the contractors who formed the East Wing. The contractors lived in the better furnished, front part of the association building, while the craftsmen were crammed together in the back portion.

East and West met around the turn of the century, after the workers pressed for more benefits - thus the *Lo Pan Ku Miou,* the temple of the contractors, became the *Lo Pan Hang,* a joint association temple. Several unaffiliated builders' and contractors' associations have since been formed in Penang.

The Carpenter's Guild was undermined when modern building techniques were introduced, which allowed contractors to use wage labour to raise concrete buildings. Western-trained architects superseded traditional master builders.

A few skilled woodcarvers have been absorbed by the furniture workshops such as *Wah Dah* on Burmah Road.

However, the majority of the craftsmen who created Penang's heritage buildings have since adapted, retired, gone into maintenance work or unrelated trades, and have had litte opportunity to train another generation to carry on their traditional skills.

designed a flying machine - giant kites which allowed spies to glide over enemy territory. His genius as an inventor was not missed by the government of his time, who recruited him as a military engineer.

An old couplet portrays Lo Pan as a moral teacher. "I invented the rule and compass to formulate the square and the round, I invented the nib and straight thread to teach future generations the straight and the level".

The right-angle rule draws a square, which represents propriety. The compass draws a circle which represents equality, since all points in the circle are equi-distant from the centre. Together, the square and the round symbolize manners and morality. With these two instruments, he also standardized the hand cart.

The nib and straight thread refers to the *bak thau,* a simple device used to draw a straight line with an inked thread. The ruler uses a traditional measure which is roughly equivalent to 1 1/4 inches. The sections of the measure signify life, old age, illness and death. Hence "the level and the straight" is a metaphor for the origin and nature of man.

The Carpenter's Guild, Love Lane. The reroofing and pilot phase of the restoration was completed by the Penang Heritage Trust in the year 2000.

LUMUT LANE

SHEIKH ZACHARIAH BASHEER & SONS

Sheikh Zachariah continued to be a leader of the Acheen Street community after the death of his father Sheikh Omar (see also Acheen Street). In 1900, he established the commission agency at Lumut Lane. In the 1920s they traded in rubber, copra, pepper, betelnuts, coffee, cloves, nutmegs, benjamin, gambier and shells.

His son-in-law and sons became highly successful "pilgrim brokers", arranging pilgrim travel to Mecca. Many houses along Acheen Street, Armenian Street and Kampong Kolam were at one time or other used for lodging the pilgrims.

Dato' Haji Fathil Basheer, son of Sheikh Zachariah, was born here 1899.

The writer Ahmad Rashid Talu, a prodigy of Syed Sheikh Al-Hadi, was also born in this house in 1889 (see also Jelutong Road). His work *Iakah Salmah?* published in 1928 was the first Malay novel featuring a local setting and local characters.

MACALISTER ROAD

Colonel Norman Macalister was Colonel Commander of the Artillery Detachment and a close confidante of Captain Light. He later became Governor of Penang (1807-1811).

Macalister Road offers a pleasant drive shaded by mature Angsana trees. Along the western section of Macalister Road is a turn-of-the-century European suburb with grand houses such as *Mayfair* and *Union Villa* (formerly Crosby Hall), next to which is the the State Guest House *(Rumah Tetamu)*, formerly the first Chief Minister's official residence.

The eastern section of Macalister Road has rather fewer old trees. The King Edward Memorial Hospital built in the 1910s was the first Maternity Hospital in Penang. The hospital was relocated after the war; the premises are now held in trust by the Municipal Council and rented to non-profit organisations.

Below, formerly Sheikh Zachariah Basheer & Sons. Above, the Baobab tree.

There are two important mosques at this end. The first is the Simpang Enam Mosque built by a diamond merchant Haji Abdul Wahab in 1893. *Simpang Enam* is the junction of six roads, one of which has been removed by the Komtar development.

The second is the Pakistani Mosque, built after the war, when there was a great influx of northern Indian Muslims due to the civil war in India.

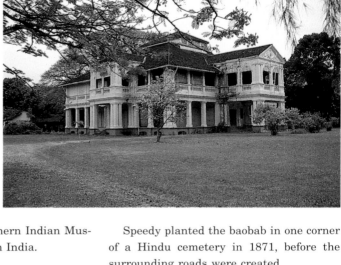

THE BAOBAB TREE

Captain Speedy, the soldier of fortune who recruited Sikh soldiers for the Menteri of Larut, was known for his adventures in Abyssinia, from whence came Penang's oldest baobab tree (see also Sikh Temple, Brick Kiln Road).

Speedy planted the baobab in one corner of a Hindu cemetery in 1871, before the surrounding roads were created.

This particular baobab tree is the mother plant of all baobabs in Malaysia. Its preservation was argued in the meetings of the City Council of the 1930s. The elephantine tree is carefully propped up, and may yet live out its maximum life span of two millenia!

PHILOMATIC SOCIETY

The *Sio Lan Teng* was a Chinese Merchant's Club where Dr. Sun Yat Sen delivered his first speech in Penang in 1906, to a most unsympathetic audience.

The Nanyang Chinese were then divided into two camps - the reformists who thought China could be saved by introducing a parliamentary system and a constitutional monarchy, and the revolutionaries who wanted to bring down the

Two mansions in the Macalister Road suburbs. Above, Crosby Hall, also known as Union Villa. Below, Mayfair, now a private school.

Manchu dynasty and establish a Republic.

After the Canton Uprising in the spring of 1911, the tide of opinion swung toward the revolutionaries. Many reformists publicly severed their Manchu queues as they changed sides (see also Armenian Street).

The revolutionaries won in 1911, and Dr. Sun's supporters bought

over the *Sio Lan Teng* premises and used it for the Philomatic Society, a reading club started by the Tung Meng Hooi.

For some years, it housed the Chung Ling School and the Fukien Girls' School, now the Penang Chinese Girls' School. The schools were started in 1917 and 1919 respectively by Tan Sin Cheng and others key members of the Tung Meng Hooi.

Today, the premises are used by a private school. A large oil painting of Dr. Sun Yat Sen still hangs in the front hall.

MADRAS LANE

HU YEW SEAH

By the turn of the century, there were already a number of English-educated Chinese, typically the Baba or Straits Chinese elite, who grew up in ignorance of their mother tongue.

Choong Thiam Poe, an early member of the Tung Meng Hui (see also Armenian Street), was formally educated at Penang Free School but had the opportunity to learn Chinese language and literature through home tuition. He founded the Hu Yew Seah to offer Mandarin classes, so that his fellow Babas would not miss out on their linguistic heritage.

The premises in Madras Lane were inaugurated by Rabindranath Tagore when he visited

Above, the Philomatic Society building and below, the Hu Yew Seah - both started by Tung Meng Hooi members.

MAGAZINE ROAD

The government gunpowder depot stood at the junction of *Simpang Enam* (at the site of Gama).

The *Tao Bo Keong* temple here is the focus of the *Kew Ong Iah* or Nine Emperor Gods Festival (see also Kuan Yin See, Burmah Road). The mediums perform a variety of pain-defying feats during the nine-day celebrations (late October or early November).

Magazine Road is the first of seven parallel roads comprising the first properly planned urban residential quarter. The terrace houses catered mostly to the Chinese middle-class and those built in the 1920s-30s are good examples of late Straits Eclectic style.

Magazine Road is called *Kuay Ka Ngah Thau Teow Lor* (First Street after the Prangin Creek). Likewise, the Chinese street names for the adjacent Noordin Street, Presgrave Street, Tye Sin Street, Macallum Street, Katz Street and Sandilands Street refer to their order of development.

Penang in 1927. The Nobel Prize winning poet was a great hero among the English-speaking literati in Asia.

Hu Yew Seah's long-term patron was Dr. Wu Lien Teh, the internationally-renowned "Plague Fighter" who combatted the dreaded Manchurian Plague in 1911 and wrote the standard work "Pathological Findings in Pneumonic Plague".

As one of the early Queen's Scholars from Penang Free School, Dr. Wu studied medicine at Cambridge. He later led the major reform and social movements of his time - the Penang Anti-Opium Association, the Confucian Revival Movement, the World's Chinese Students' Federation and the Straits Chinese British Association.

Above, Madras Lane. Below, typical terrace houses in the seven streets south of the Prangin Creek.

HUI AUN KONG HOOI

When this Hokkien district association was founded in 1914, its members were typically poor trishawmen, mechanics and construction workers. Among them were a group of women construction labourers (see picture of Bridge Street godowns).

Today many of its members have emerged as wealthy developers and towkays in the transport industry - the most famous being Tan Sri Loh Boon Siew, the "Honda tycoon".

The Art Deco building from 1938 has a spacious hall with a black-and-white chequered floor. The association's lion dance troupe, which is among the best in Penang, practises here several times a week.

MALAY STREET

Malay Street is a charming residential street with some fine late 19th century Chinese elite shophouses. Before that, it was part of the mid-19th century Malay town south of Acheen Street - cows were then bred and slaughtered here, hence the Chinese name *Thai Gu Au* (Cow-Slaughtering Street).

Above, Malay Street. Below, The Hui Aun Association building. The adjacent shophouse depicts the late Straits Eclectic "sugar icing" decoration, typical of the Magazine Road facades.

MARKET STREET

Market Street today is musical, colourful, aromatic and animated. Here you will find incense, spices, garlands, stone implements, food, sarees, peacock feathers, religious paraphernalia as well as portraits of Hindu gods and Hindustani film stars.

Today, the shops and eating-places along Market Street itself are mostly run by Hindus, while Tamil Muslim shopkeepers abound along the perpendicular streets.

Market Street lies within Light's original grid. The Tamils call this historic centre *Kadai Teru* (Street of Shops) while the British called it *Chola Place* or *Little Madras*. Several years ago, a local cultural committee renamed it *Little India,* and the name has caught on.

Some of the single-storey shops here were built with the remains of the St. Xavier's Institution (see also Farquhar Street). The late Mr. Yeoh Seng Chan told of how he made money just after the war with a bright recyling idea - salvaging bricks from the destroyed school building to reconstruct the bombed-out area in Market Street.

The old market used to be situated at Market Street Ghaut, at the present site of the Victoria Street bus station and hawker complex (see also Che Em Lane).

Scenes from Market Street.

MUNTRI STREET

The words "minister" and "mandarin" are both related to the Malay word *Muntri* or *Menteri*. There is a theory that Muntri Street was named after the famous Mantri of Larut Ngah Ibrahim son of Long Ja'afar, although the exact location of his residence in Penang is not known. The Mantri is credited with the development of the tin-mining district of Larut in Perak in the mid-19th century.

There are some wonderful residential shophouses from the turn of the century when Muntri Street was an elite Chinese residential area (see also the story of Chan Kim Boon, Batu Gantong).

The Lam Wah Ee Hospital in Batu Lanchang started out in Muntri Street as a hospital for the poor. Behind the Hailam Association is a small unnamed street with a traditional joss stick making shop.

Along Muntri Street are many Cantonese associations and guilds, such as the Leong See Kah Meow (Leong surname clanhouse), the Penang Restaurant and Tea Shops Association, the Penang and Province Wellesley

Cafe Association and the Tailors Assocation.

The association of *Chan, Seng, Thong, Heong* and *Wooi* surnames represent a joint association formed by small groups of Chinese with these surnames in Penang. A look at the pictures hanging on the wall reveal that the members are predominantly *amahs*.

In the 1930s, these Cantonese women migrated in waves to Malaya and Singapore to work for wealthy European and Chinese households.

The "black-and-white" Cantonese amahs had impeccable reputations as live-in nannies, servants and cooks. Upright and frugal, they wore a uniform of white top and

Above, the Cantonese amahs playing a card game called Chit Kee in their Kongsi Pang. Below, elegant shophouse facade along Muntri Street.

deity of goldsmiths.

The Hailam Association & Temple

The Temple of the Heavenly Queen, or *Thean Ho Keong*, is dedicated to Mar Chor, patron deity of seafarers. The Hailam temple was founded before 1866 and the present building dates from 1895.

Two interesting features are the altar of Kwan Kong raised over the inner portal, and the pillars cut in Sung dynasty style. Goats are slaughtered in offering to the goddess on her birthday.

The Hailams (also called Hainanese) hail from the island of Hainan in South China. In Penang, the men have traditionally worked as cooks (see also Loke Thye Kee Restaurant, Burmah Road and Wing Look Restaurant, Penang Road).

In 1925, the association's name was changed to *Kheng Chew Hoay Kuan,* reflecting the official name change of the Hailam province. The association school, *Aik Hua,* was built in 1905 and extended in 1919.

black pants, keeping their own moral code, forswearing marriage and family life to join the sisterhood.

Careers as overseas amahs were an alternative to the peasant's life in China and potential oppression by husbands and mother-in-laws. Peasant women from Sun Tak distrct already had a tradition of independence as silk industry workers and vegetarian nuns (see also Sun Tak Association, Love Lane).

The amahs in Penang regularly remitted money to poor relatives in China through the agency of professional letter-writers.

The last generation of amahs have reached old age, some have returned to China. In between jobs and in their retirement, the amahs stay in shared quarters *(Kongsi Pang)* in the Muntri Street area - which includes Stewart Lane, Love Lane, Muda Lane and Market Lane - close to their Goddess of Mercy Temple.

The Goldsmith's Association

Ta Kam Hong, founded in 1832, is the oldest and largest association of goldsmiths in Malaysia. The present guild temple was built in 1903 and dedicated to Wu Ching, the patron

Above, the Hailam Association Temple. Below, the Goldsmith's Association.

KING WAN ASSOCIATION

The first union of Chinese shopkeepers and clerical workers in Penang was founded in 1923 to fight for non-working Sundays and better salaries. It was banned after a workers' strike. In 1926, the union was revived with the name *King Wan,* which means "Warning the Stubborn".

NORTHAM ROAD

Growing up in Penang one cannot help but hear about the decadent lifestyles of the rich and famous who lived and revelled along "Millionaire's Row". The Chinese remember it as the *Ang Mo Lor* (European Road) because of the *Ang Mor Lau* (European bungalows) there.

Northam Road begins where the colonial cemetery was established just outside of the limits of the 18th century town.

This was the first residential suburb where the elite had their homes along the scenic North Beach. Among them were the early colonial administrators - Raffles lived in *The Runnymede* and Anson in *Peninsula Cottage.* The Penang Club founded in the 1860s was the most exclusive on the settlement.

The Kedah Sultan has maintained a residence at Northam Road for over a century (see also Udini Road). Among the first non-Europeans to move into the neighbourhood, at the turn of the century were the Noordin family at *Clifton,* and the Khaw brothers of South Thailand at *Chakrabong House, Asdang House, Hardwicke* and *Brook Lodge.*

Each mansion was set in ample gardens that came with tennis courts, stables, circular driveways, service buildings and sea walls which had to be maintained at high cost against an eroding shoreline. The pretty bou-

---

Above, spring-cleaning day for the Cantonese amahs at the Kongsi Pang next door to the King Wan association.

ladder through dint of hard work, somehow managed to combine frugality with the required ostentation, only to have their hard-earned wealth squandered by playboy sons with a penchant for fast women and slow horses.

High living and the Depression of the 1930s steadily devoured the vast family fortunes. The Second World War swept away the remainder. Houses were looted and emptied of their valuable contents. Within a few years, much wealth was dissipated to feed the numerous dependants and hangers-on. The oversized family jewels worn by the Nyonyas were dismembered and traded for some of the comforts to which the gentle-born were accustomed to.

After the war, some currencies and deposits had become worthless. The most substantial assets which had not been taken away during the war were lands and houses - the large family mansions, the holiday homes, the terrace house properties.

Members of large extended households who lived in harmony under the same roof during better times now came back to fight over what was left of the family fortunes.

THE PROTESTANT CEMETERY

Francis Light died of frustration, overwork and fever, and was buried in the Protestant Cemetery in 1794. Among those who share this graveyard are several Governors of the Settlement including Phillip Dundas (d. 1807), William Petrie (d. 1816) and Colo-

levard, through which were driven the gilded horse carriages and later the fancy cars, was lined with shady trees and wide grassy banks.

By the early 20th century, it was no longer the Europeans who lived there but the self-made local millionaires with multiple wives, and eclectic mansions fine enough for entertaining their European friends.

In these homes were floors of Carrara marble, Czechoslovakian chandeliers, late Victorian cast iron porches, Chinese mother-of-pearl inlaid blackwood sets and Burmese teak cupboards filled with Nyonya ware and English porcelain dolls. The ultimate in snobbery was to enjoy a class reversal by employing European butlers and horsemen.

For the sons and daughters of the elite, the 1920s was an era of world-touring, endless partying and holidaying in each other's hill and seaside resorts. The men took easily to bar-hopping and mistress-swapping. The women pursued their liberation just as avidly, leaving their offspring to the care of black-and-white nannies.

It was a notorious syndrome of many elite Chinese families of that era - the first generation climbed to the top of the social

The Yeoh Cheang Seng Villa from 1913.

nel John Alexander Bannerman (d. 1819), all of whom died in office.

Here also lies Raffles' brother-in-law, Quintin Dick Thomas (d. 1809), and men who had contributed greatly to the settlement such as Light's trading partner, James Scott (d. 1808), David Brown of Glugor Estate (d. 1825) and Penang's foremost man of letters, James Richardson Logan (d. 1869).

The resting place of Reverend Hutchings is visited annually on the 21st of October by the senior class of Penang Free School who traditionally drink a toast over his grave on Founder's Day (see also State Museum, Farquhar Street).

Early death and the untimely loss of their loved ones was the price many pioneer settlers had to pay. Unsanitary conditions and tropical illnesses such as malaria and cholera claimed the lives of both the young and old, including innumerable infants and moth-ers who died at childbirth.

The cemetery was a mound at the edge of the early town. The wall was built and the cemetery consecrated around 1818. On the other side of the southern wall is a Roman Catholic cemetery (see also St. Xavier's Church, Penang Road)

The Protestant burial ground was closed towards the end of the 19th century and further burials were located at the Western Road cemetery. Many graves and memorials were destroyed when Japanese bombs fell in the eastern and western ends of the cemetery.

Frangipani trees create a shaded aisle through the burial ground which is full of timeless forms such as broken columns, Greek urns, Roman sarcophagi and structures emulating the canopied tombs of Indian rajahs.

Some dedications to members of the East India Company were written by their fellow-

The Protestant Cemetery.

officers in Calcutta, where the marble gravestones were engraved and despatched to this settlement.

There are also graves of settlers, shipmen, or passing travellers inscribed in Dutch, French and German. Over thirty Chinese graves which date from the 1860s to 1880s are suspected to have belonged to Taiping Christians who sought refuge in the Nanyang.

In 1859, when officer Thomas Leonowens died at the age of 31, he left a young widow. Stranded in the East, Anna sought employment as a schoolmistress in Siam, and subsequently wrote about her experience. The dry memoirs of the schoolmistress received scant attention, but several decades later someone else rewrote her story as a popular book for schoolgirls. The experience of Anna Leonowens, whose husband lies buried in the Protestant Cemetery, was finally adapted to the popular musical "The King and I".

RUNNYMEDE

Raffles came to Penang in 1805 as Assistant Secretary to the Governor and was based here until 1811. In the first year, he earned a salary of 6,000 Spanish Dollars per annum, of which he paid 300 pounds rent for a brick bungalow called *Runnymede,* and sent 400 pounds home to his mother. Raffles and Olivia also had a hill house at Mount Olivia overlooking the north beach.

Penang was then regarded as a health resort for British Indian officers, and so in 1805, a slightly ill John Caspar Leyden came to convalesce. During his ten week stay, the assistant surgeon became good friends with Raffles and his wife, and was later to recommend Raffles to the Governor-General of India, Lord Minto (see also Government House, Light Street).

The Runnymede Hotel, established at the turn of the century in Raffles' brick bungalow, was ravaged by fire in 1921. The original bungalow seems to have survived, though badly damaged and awkwardly incorporated into the present Runnymede complex.

The hotel was subsequently expanded and run by two Scotsmen, Foster and Parker. The large seafront wing was built in the 1930s.

The 1930s wing, with sea-facing rooms each with private bathroom and sitting area. Below, the old Runnymede building with one side removed.

The large ballroom accommodated 150 people and opened out to the casurarina-lined lawn. An orchestra played daily; dances were held twice a week and when liners were in port.

By the end of the decade, the Runnymede had 70 rooms compared to the 71 rooms of its chief rival, the Eastern & Oriental Hotel. The

Runnymede management had also taken over the Crag Hotel in Penang Hill from the Sarkies brothers.

The British army later requisitioned it for a transit camp and officers' mess. After Independence, the building became a government Rest & Recreation Centre known as *Wisma Persekutuan*. It is now the base of the Malaysian Second Army Infantry Division.

SHIH CHUNG SCHOOL

Inspired by the Raffles in Singapore, the Tye brothers opened their own hotel in the 1910s called *Raffles-by-the-Sea,* just across the road from the Runnymede Hotel.

Tea was taken on the lawn of this striking pagoda-shaped building, of a unique architectural style which can only be described as Anglo-Chinese.

When built in the 1880s by Cheah Tek Soon (after whom Tek Soon Street was named), it was the first five-storey residence in Penang - the landmark

is still called *Goh Chan Lau*. When his brother Cheah Tek Thye lived here in the 1900s, it was called the *Chinese Residency*.

The building later served as the premises of the P'i Joo Girls' School, the Government Girls' School and finally the Shih Chung Branch School.

The five-storey building has since been stripped of its cast iron fittings and renovated into a three storey-building with a jack roof. The front hall, which is twice the normal ceiling height, has extraordinarily large woodcarved panels that would have truly impressed visitors to the Chinese Residency.

Above, Shih Chung School in session. Below, the Palladian pagoda.

HARDWICKE

A former resident of this early 19th century bungalow created a mosaic of the Star of
India embedded in the floor of the side hall,
using shards of Dutch plates.

At the turn of the century, Khaw Joo Ghee
of the famous Khaw family used it as his
residence. He then sold it to Lim Cheng Ean,
a prominent lawyer who served as the first
Chinese Magistrate in Penang (see also Phuah
Hin Leong Road).

Educated at Clare College, Cambridge,
Cheng Ean became a prominent lawyer and

the first Chinese magistrate in Penang.

As a member of Legislative Council of the
Straits Settlements, Cheng Ean was an out-
spoken champion of causes such as vernacular education and freedom of the press.

He took over *Hardwicke* in the 1920s and
added to it the heraldic lions and emblems of
his beloved college. A recluse toward the end
of his life, he retired to his Claremont Estate
in Penang Hill.

SOONSTEAD

Heah Swee Lee, a wealthy planter and
Perak State Councillor, built *Northam Lodge*
in the 1910s. It was later sold to his in-laws
and renamed *Soonstead*.

The Penang Polo Ground was donated by
Swee Lee, who became the first non-European member of the Polo Club.

His son Heah Seng Hye did one better by
becoming the first non-European Captain
and playing with HRH The Prince of Wales at

Above, Hardwicke at the corner of Northam Road and Pangkor Road. The grounds have some mature trees.
Below, highly artistic, flowing stucco.

the Selangor Club, Kuala Lumpur in 1922.

Swee Lee's sons indulged in adventurous hobbies - one was a game hunter and taxidermist, another pioneered Penang's first wireless station. Heah Seng Hong, an amateur pilot and photographer, took many excellent pictures of his family and the mansion, including interior shots and aerial views.

ASDANG HOUSE

At the turn of the century, Penang was a bustling metropolis compared to provincial South Thailand. The Khaw family, as Governors of South Thailand, entertained their distinguished Thai friends and dignitaries at their stately homes in Penang.

On his return from Europe in 1890, the Prince Chulalongkorn was welcomed by Khaw Sim Bee and a delegation of Malay princes and noblemen from Kedah and Perlis at a reception in *Chakrabong House,* formerly on the Northam Road beach front.

In October 1929, Sim Bee's nephew Khaw Joo Tock had the King and Queen of Siam for lunch at his new bungalow on Penang Hill and then for tea at *Asdang House*, a "flamboyant mansion of Moorish design".

A frequent guest to *Asdang House* was Prince Damrong Rajanubhab who wrote about the Khaw family in his book *History of Ranong* in 1928 (see also Koe Guan office, Beach Street).

THE ALOES

Among the original European residences along Northam Road were Anglo-Indian bungalows like *The Aloes,* built in the early 19th century. Like the original *Runnymede,* this house has a double porch - one facing the road and another facing the sea.

Middle left, Northam Lodge also known as Soonstead. Above right, Asdang House, in later years known as the Metropole Hotel (demolished). Below, the Aloes.

WOODVILLE

Lim Lean Teng, a Teochew planter with vast estates in Kedah, is best remembered as the founder of Han Chiang School in Penang and the main benefactor to the Nanyang University Library in Singapore.

He wanted a mansion with a dome like like that of the former Hongkong & Shanghai Bank building on Beach Street. The architect Charles Miller obliged with this 1925 creation. *Woodville* is still owned and maintained by the Lim family today.

LEONG YIN KEAN MANSION

This compact palace was the fancy of a young man who fell in love with Italy. Leong Yin Kean, son of tin-miner Leong Fee (see also Leith Street) and a student at Cambridge, also had country homes in Penang Hill named *Tosari* and *Lausanne*.

The architect of this mansion was Charles Miller of the firm of Stark & McNeill, who also designed *Woodville*.

Built for a quarter of a million Straits Dollars in 1926, it incorporated panels and floors of Neapolitan mosaic. The furniture was manufactured in Bangkok according to the specifications and oil sketches of an Italian interior designer.

Leong Yin Kean, an amateur pilot, salvaged the wooden propeller of his plane after a flying accident and displayed it in his living room. After his death, his two daughters stayed on until the 1980s.

Above, Woodville. Below, part of the Leong Yin Kean Mansion (now beautifully refurbished into a restaurant and corporate office).

HOMESTEAD

In 1918, Lim Chin Guan replaced Quah Beng Kee as Managing Director of Eastern Shipping. The two were life-long rivals, and Lim Chin Guan apparently wanted to block Beng Kee's view of the sea, from *Columbia Lodge* (now Maple Gold club premises).

Homestead was thus built with a handsome colonnade breasting its expansive frontage. It was designed by James Stark of Stark & McNeil in 1919 for Chin Guan's father, Lim Mah Chye. A small theatre with a high stage was also built at the back.

The mansion was later acquired by Yeap Chor Ee, founder of the Ban Hin Lee Bank, who provided for its upkeep in his trust (see also Ban Hin Lee Bank, Beach Street). Homestead was one of the few mansions that survived the war relatively intact.

Today, Homestead is still the elegant residence of Yeap Chor Ee's descendants.

Above, the Leong Yin Kean Mansion. Below, Homestead, one of the best-maintained historic mansions in Penang today.

137

Before the European mining companies ventured into Perak, the industry was largely financed by Penang *towkays* and the labour controlled by the Penang-based secret societies. The Ghee Hin and Hai San secret societies fought a bitter war over the tin-mines, each aligning itself with a Malay contender for the rule of Larut and its mining rights.

PANGKOR ROAD

The important Pangkor Treaty of 1874 settled two decades of feuds over the tin-mines in Larut. It also marked the beginning of British intervention in the Malay states.

The potential for tin-mining in Larut, a district of Perak, was first recognized by Che Long Jaafar, who took out a title around 1850. At first the tin was mainly exported to China, where the metal was used to make silver-stamped joss paper. Then the mass production of canned food created a world demand for tin.

One of the first actions of Sir Andrew Clarke as Governor of the Straits Settlements was to negotiate an end to the disputes. At a conference held on Pangkor island, 26 headmen signed the Pangkor engagement, with Chung Keng Kooi representing the Hai San society and Chin Ah Yam representing the Ghee Hin (see also Church Street and Rope Walk).

The Pangkor Treaty signed on the same day recognized the Raja Muda Abdullah as Sultan of Perak, thus ignoring the claims of his enemy, the Mantri of Larut (see Muntri Street).

The tin-mining areas awarded to the Hai San were superior, to the disgust of the Ghee Hin who eventually evacuated Larut. The Ghee Hin went on to develop the tin rich Kinta Valley and to build the town of Ipoh. The Hai San stayed in Larut and continued to develop the old town of Taiping.

Years later, the disused tin-mines of the Hai San were donated to the Municipality and transformed into the Taiping Lakes.

Above, Rain Trees along Pangkor Road, below left, gate posts along Pangkor Road.

PEEL AVENUE

Sir Wiliam Peel was acting Resident Councillor in Penang in 1917 and Chief Secretary to the Government of the Federated Malay States from 1928-30.

· Peel Avenue is an extension of Pangkor Road, cutting through marshy grounds and a lake in the early 20th century. It is lined with Cuban Royal Palms planted in 1935.

PENANG ROAD

Penang Road was the first road that extended out of George Town. Today, in a supreme accomplishment of traffic planning, it has been carefully dissected to channel traffic flow to and from all directions.

Several bygone communities which settled along this early road are remembered by street names - the north Sumatrans at *Kampong Deli,* the Malabaris at *Kampong Malabar* and the Bihar community at Sri Bahari Road. Near Sri Bahari Road was also the Ambonese community, remembered by

the local place name *Kampong Ambon.*

In the early 19th century, Penang Road was lined with Indian Muslim shops; most of these gave way to Chinese businesses at the turn of the century.

The entrance to *Kampong Deli* is flanked by two bungalows disguised as shophouses. An occupant of one of them is the old *Kek Seng* coffeeshop, which sells its own brand of corn and durian-flavoured home-made ice-cream.

A landmark along Penang Road is the Police Headquarters along Dickens Street, erected by Malabari construction workers. The massive building had just been completed when Japanese bombs were dropped on it. The bombing was felt and reported in the nearby Straits Echo building at the corner of Dato' Koya Road.

Above, Cuban Palms along Peel Avenue. Below, the roofscapes of George Town. Note the Anglo-Indian bungalow, now occupied by Ai Goh Hotel, concealed behind a row of shophouses along Penang Road.

monument which cannot be ignored. It was designed by Dato' Lim Chong Keat, brother of the former Chief Minister Tun Dr. Lim Chong Eu. The late Buckminster Fuller was consultant for the Geodesic Dome.

Three tiers of government are housed in this 65-storey building. Both public and private sector offices are located in the

Among the journalists then working at the Straits Echo were Dato' Khor Cheang Kee, Tan Sri Lee Siew Yee and the Ceylonese editor Saravanamuttu Manicasothy (d. 1974) who later wrote the book "The Sara Saga".

Sara took charge of the situation as president of the Penang Services Committee. The British had evacuated Penang at the outbreak of war in 1941, and it was up to the committee to maintain order and public services, while calling an end to the bombing.

Penang Road was a major shopping area in the 1970s, known for emporia and early department stores. Today, it is still a good place to shop for photographic supplies, consumer goods, souvenirs and local foodstuffs.

The *Penang Bazaar* is an old theatre hall converted into a den of bargain stalls. Antique and curio shops are concentrated on the northern end of Penang Road.

KOMTAR, which stands for Komplex Tun Abdul Razak, is a

tower, whereas the podium is a large shopping mall. The Viewing Gallery on the 57th Floor enables one to have a magnificent view of the historic roofscapes of George Town.

Terra cotta roofs were already evident in George Town by the first quarter of the 19th century. Though commonly known as "Chinese clay tiles", these Mediterranean type tiles were probably introduced by the Portuguese to the region.

For over one and a half centuries, George Town's roof tiles and bricks were mainly produced in the kilns of Sungai Dua, a small

Above, the Grand Parade along Penang Road, in front of a shopping emporium. Below, the building of the former Straits Echo.

town near Butterworth on mainland Penang. The kilns are located by the Prai River, where there are clay deposits.

WING LOOK RESTAURANT

Hainanese-type Western food is the speciality of Wing Look, the first Western-style restaurant run by Chinese management. This corner building is part of Khoo Sian Ewe's complex (see also Loke Thye Kee, Burmah Road).

Hainanese men worked as cooks in European households and created local Western dishes like Chicken Chop, Pork Chop, *Kay Se Tu* (Chicken Stew) and *Bak Se-Tek* (Pork Steak).

Wing Look was one of the favourite restaurants of the late Tunku Abdul Rahman (see also Ayer Rajah Road). During the Japanese Occupation, it served as a canteen which catered exclusively to the Admiral and high-ranking officers of the Japanese Navy.

ST. XAVIER'S CHURCH

Behind the Catholic Information Centre is the St. Francis Xavier's Church founded in 1852 primarily for Tamil-speaking Christians. Part of this complex is the St. Joseph's Orphanage and a school. The church building has an unusual ceiling woven out of *mengkuang* or screwpine leaves.

Some of the Holy Infant Jesus Sisters who established the Convent Light Street are buried at the Roman Catholic cemetery, which is linked to the more well-known Protestant Cemetery on the other side of the wall.

SEH ONG KONGSI

The *Kai Meng Ong Beow* is dedicated to the "pioneer-king", who led the Chinese to settle in South China in the late Tang dynasty and thus became the first *Ong* of the Hokkien state - the surname Ong being the equivalent of *King* or *Koenig*. The association was founded by three brothers in the 1890s.

Above, Wing Look restaurant. Below, the Ong Kongsi.

PENANG STREET

The section between Light Street and Bishop Street is called *Kau Keng Choo* because there were originally nine elite shophouses which had a second front at King Street.

The Straits Chinese who used to live here, close to Light Street, were also relatively Westernised in taste. At the turn of the century, they set the trend for High Straits Eclecticism, which was later emulated all over town.

In one of these houses today is Ganesh

Press, which has a fantastic collection of early printing and binding machines, including lead types for Roman, Jawi, Tamil and Chinese characters. Next to it is a shophouse which still has its original woodcarved doors and Art Nouveau tiles. The Gujerati family who lives there maintains a private Hindu temple dedicated to the goddess Durga.

The section between Bishop and Market Streets was called *Macao Ke* or *Thong Yan Kay* (Cantonese Street), reflecting the predominance of Cantonese shopkeepers there. Here is the *Seh Mui Kongsi,* a clan association whose members are predominantly of the Sing Ling dialect group.

The southern section of Penang Street is more Indian in character. Along this street are several "banana leaf rice" restaurants, where rice, pickles and curries are served on banana leaf and eaten by hand.

KWANGTUNG & TENGCHEW ASSOCIATION

When founded in 1801, this Cantonese association brought together the committee that had been organising the Hungry Ghosts Festival at the Goddess of Mercy Temple since 1796, and the trustee board of the "White Cloud Mountain" (*Pek Hoon Sua*) cemeteries at Mount Erskine Road.

The present building of Shanghai-style Art Deco was designed by Boutcher in 1938. The building plan can be seen hanging inside just by the entrance.

Above, door to one of the "Nine Houses". Below, the Shanghai Art Deco architecture of the Kwangtung & Tengchew Association building.

ANGLO-INDIAN GODOWN

There used to be many such corner godowns in the commercial town, near the port area. This is Penang's best surviving example, dating from early to mid-19th century. "Godown", from the Malay word *gudang*, is an Anglo-Indian term for a warehouse.

The Anglo-Indian style building has a tall storage space with columns at ground level, and quarters and offices on the upper floor. Its proportions are similar to that of the Government House (see Convent Light Street) and can be also compared to the Gedung Raja Abdullah in Klang from 1857.

YIN OI TONG

The traditional Chinese medical hall, established by a Hakka medicine-pedlar at Pitt Street in 1796, is the oldest in Southeast Asia. After the Yin Oi Tong moved to Penang Street, it continued to retain its original postal address - P.O. Box No. 1, Penang.

KOIL VIDHU

The *chettiar* belongs to a clan from Tamil Nadu, whose menfolk are money-lenders by occupation. They adhere to their own moral, religious and business codes. In India they live in a *chettinar* or chettiar area, around their Murugan temple.

Known for their frugal way of life, the chettiars conduct their transactions over a low wooden desk, with both parties seated on the floor.

They have been called the "Jews of the

Above, the Anglo-Indian Godown. Middle right, an Indian banana leaf rice restaurant.

143

patrons of the silver chariot procession. The silver chariot conveys their deity Lord Murugan from the Koil Vidhu to the Nattukkottai Chettiar Temple (see also Waterfall Road). For the rest of the year, the chariot is stored in a historic garage in Penang Street opposite the Koil Vidhu.

P. RAMLEE ROAD

P. RAMLEE HOUSE

The legendary P. Ramlee was Malaysia's most loved performer (1928-1973). P. Ramlee was a director, actor, writer, musician, composer, arranger and the foremost figure in the country's film and music industry.

East", for as money-lenders they are found in most large towns throughout Southeast and East Asia. As a group, they own much property in Penang, including many houses which were forfeited through mortgages.

P. Ramlee alias Teuku Zakariah, was the son of Teuku Nyak Puteh from Aceh. He attended a Malay school in Kampong Jawa and then the Penang Free School.

Since 1850, the chettiars have had their clan association and Hindu temple in the southern end of Penang Street. This section was often called "Chetty Street"; the Chinese and Malay street names also correspond. The old building was bombed during the Second World War, and rebuilt on the same site. The original idols were saved and reinstalled.

While growing up, he learnt to sing Malay and Tamil songs, and became involved with a local Bangsawan troupe. He scored a music hit with his first composition *Azizah*. At the age of 20, he left home to find work in the film industry in Singapore.

During Thaipusam (late January or early February), the chettiars are the

Above, the Silver Chariot's garage. Below, the Ariff Mosque.

The house where P. Ramlee was born was reconstructed on the same site and turned into a historic personality museum. Established by the National Archives, the museum features biographical information, artefacts and educational displays related to the artist's early years in Penang.

THE JAPANESE CEMETERY

Penang had a small Japanese community concentrated around Kampung Malabar and Cintra Street (see also Cintra Street). This cemetery has several dozen graves from the early 20th century and the Second World War. The Japanese Cemetery is located right next to P. Ramlee's house.

PERAK ROAD

Along Perak Road are many traditional Malay, Peranakan Jawi and Chinese villages. Some Tamil Muslims who traded with the interior during the early years intermarried with the local women and settled down at *Kampong Dodol* and other villages around the Pinang river.

Several Indian Muslim mosques were built - proceeding from town you will pass the Khan Rajabee Mosque, the Rawana Mosque, the Hashim Yahaya Mosque and the Ariff Mosque on your right.

The Perak Road cemetery is the largest Muslim burial ground on the island (see also Campbell Street). Graves are visited and cleaned during Hari Raya Puasa and Hari Raya Haji.

Here are the mausoleums of Dato Kramat (see also Dato Kramat Road) and Sheikh Abdul Ghani from Madura who is better known as *Tuan Guru* (see also Acheen Street).

ARIFF MOSQUE

This mosque was built in the 1920s by Ariff Wanchee Ariffin Mohamed, in memory of his father Mohamed Ariff bin Mohamed Tajoodin (see also Hutton Lane).

Ariff Wanchee was an English-educated *alim* (an authority on Muslim law). He also donated land to the Municipality, now the site of Ariffin Road and Ariffin Court.

Above, the P. Ramlee House. Below, Dato Kramat's Tomb.

STATE CHINESE PENANG ASSOCIATION

Founded in 1920 as the Straits Chinese British Association, it was one of the three organisations which were considered by the colonial authorities to represent the Chinese community - the other two being the Chinese Town Hall and Chinese Chambers of Commerce.

After the war, the association evolved into a cultural and recreational society whose main objectives are to perpetuate the traditions of the Straits Chinese or Baba Nyonya community.

Ordinarily, it celebrates Chinese New Year, Chap Goh Meh and the Mid-Autumn Festival, and also holds cooking, dancing, beadwork and embroidery classes from time to time. The SCPA moved into their present premises at 13, Perak Road in the mid-1980s. It was responsible for reviving the Baba Nyonya wedding tradition in 1987.

PHUAH HIN LEONG ROAD

Phuah Hin Leong, born to a poor Lim family, was given to a Phuah family for adoption. He was to exemplify the rags-to-riches story of the early Chinese immigrants to the Nanyang.

As one of his sons later recounted, Hin Leong started out in Penang with "a pair of oars" and ended up with a "pair of mills".

He worked as a boatman ferrying goods and passengers across the Channel. One day, two European passengers left something behind in his boat. The boatman waited for them on the same spot, forgoing the day's earnings. His honesty was rewarded with a large tip, which he frugally saved towards his own business.

This story has become urban folklore; it has been attributed to other early tycoons, and the object left behind is usually said to have been a bag of gold.

Hin Leong came to own a "a pair of mills". The first stood at the site of Komtar, in front of his house *Millview* (now Queen's Hotel) at Prangin Road, and the second at Sungai Pinang (see also Jelutong Road).

He invested in the development of many godowns along Weld Quay and Beach Street for rent to the European trading houses (see also Weld Quay). When he died in 1901, Hin Leong was thought to have been one of the wealthiest Chinese in Penang.

Against tradition, Phuah Hin Leong's children were given his original surname. Several of his sons had prominent careers between the wars; most notable were Lim

---

Another architecturally successful ensemble by Chew Eng Eam.

Cheng Teik (see also Larut Road), Lim Cheng Law, "Malaysia's most prolific contributor to newspaper postbags", Lim Cheng Ean (see Hardwicke, Northam Road) and Lim Cheng Kung, managing director of the Straits Echo.

The ensemble of terrace houses along Phuah Hin Leong Road were designed by Chew Eng Eam (see also Bangkok Lane).

PITT STREET

The world's four major religions - Christianity, Buddhism, Hinduism and Islam - are represented along this street which Light named after the then British Prime Minister, William Pitt, the Younger.

Lined up from north to south are the St. George's Church on Farquhar Street (built 1818), the Goddess of Mercy Temple (founded 1801), the Mariamman Temple on Queen Street (founded 1833) and the Kapitan Kling Mosque (founded 1801). The location of these religious institutions roughly correspond to the faiths of the various communities which settled along the adjoining east-west streets.

The wide street formerly had a market building and a police station at the centre. The spot in front of the Kapitan Kling Mosque used to be the "Auctioneer's Junction"; it is *Yeelam Muchanti* to the Tamils and *Simpang Lelong* to the Malays.

The section between Chulia and Armenian Street is still *Ia Kah* (Under the Coconut Trees) to the Chinese community.

Today, Pitt Street thrives with the activities of money-changers, jewellery and antique shops. Pitt Street has been renamed Jalan Mesjid Kapitan Keling, after the mosque rather than the man.

KAPITAN KLING MOSQUE

As soon as the East India Company stationed itself in Penang, the Muslim section of its troops comprising the Havildars, Jemadars and Sepoys founded the first mosque on the present site.

Later, the Muslim community requested their headman Cauder Mydin Merican alias Kapitan Kling to build a brick mosque.

In 1801, the government granted an 18-acre lot to the "Mohamedan Church for ever". This huge acreage was meant for the mosque and burial grounds, with surplus lands to collect rent for upkeep.

Kapitan Kling became the first Superintendent of the mosque and the appointment of the mosque officers rested with his family. He brought builders and stones from India for the project.

The original mosque was a single-storey building with minarets at each corner, with

Above, indigenous stucco motif on one of the shophouses at the section of Pitt Street called "Under the Coconut Trees". Below, flower-sellers along Pitt Street.

then the Vernacular School and finally the municipal market (see also Campbell Street).

By 1903, only eight of the 18 acres granted to the Muslim community remained as mosque property. The rest ceased to be recognized as charity land, due to improper management. Private houses encroached up to within several feet of the mosque.

In 1905 the mosque came under the administration of the Mohamedan and Hindu Endowments Board, Penang (now the State Religious Council). The mosque properties include shophouses at Chulia Street, Pitt Street, Pitt Lane, Buckingham Street and Campbell Street.

The Municipal Commission then began an extensive urban renewal programme on a scale which was unmatched in Penang until the Komtar development. Poor housing was

an outer colonnade and a low scalloped wall and granite area similar to that found in the Acheen Street Mosque.

It was surrounded by shophouses and was only accessible through narrow gateways, much like the Acheen Street Mosque and the Hokkien clan associations. The mosque was enlarged at the turn of the century into a grand and elaborate structure with minarets, turrets and domes.

Having alienated most of the town land at the beginning, the government was forced to buy back some of it at great cost for the town's social amenities.

In the 1890s, the Municipal Commission acquired a parcel of land from the Kapitan Kling Mosque estate, on which they built, first the Carnarvon Street Police Station,

Above, the Chulia Street entrance to the Kapitan Kling mosque. This mosque complex is being restored in 2001. Below, learning about Muslim heritage.

replaced by regular terrace houses designed by government-appointed architects. Roads were created through Kampong Kolam and Kampong Kaka, and Sek Chuan Lane was extended (see also Kampong Kolam).

In the 1910s, the first major renovation was carried out with funds from the Board. The architect N. A. Neubronner extended the mosque and added the Moghul domes and turrets, a large minaret for the muezzin and a *madrasah* for religious classes.

The present form was achieved after yet another extension and reroofing exercise, probably in the 1930s. The wall around the compound was built at the same time.

In a tradition which respected religious buildings, the mosque was never rebuilt, only enlarged. The minarets and alcove of the original mosque can still be seen at the back of the present mosque. The first extensions survive as the ornate inner wall of the outer aisle.

In the 1980s, the MARA building was constructed at Buckingham Street; it has not only obscured the view of the Kapitan Kling Mosque dome from Carnarvon Street, but has also cut off the mosque from the founder's tomb in Kampong Kolam.

Above, the muezzin's minaret at the junction of Buckingham Street and Pitt Street. Below, the old minaret and the quarters for mosque officials behind.

GODDESS OF MERCY TEMPLE

The temple at the end of China Street is dedicated to Kuan Yin, the Goddess of Mercy. This was the first temple built by Penang's early Chinese settlers (see also China Street).

The Kuan Yin is a Boddhisattva - a being who has actually attained Nirvana but stays behind to save those souls who have not escaped the world of suffering.

The temple is also dedicated to a second virgin goddess of mercy, *Ma Chor Poh*. The patron saint of sea voyagers, who watched over the early settlers on their dangerous journey across the South China Seas, used to have a more prominent place here.

During temple days on the first and fifteenth day of every lunar month, the place is packed with devotees, and the air thickens with incense and smoke. Oracle sticks, which correspond to standard verses, are popular with those who seek divine guidance.

The Goddess of Mercy's feast days fall on the 19th day of the second, sixth and ninth month of the lunar calendar, marking her birthday, the anniversary of her initiation, and the anniversary of attaining Nirvana.

Puppet shows and Chinese operas, sponsored by private benefactors in her honour, are staged in the granite-paved forecourt. The octagonal public well is now disused.

The temple's original name is *Kong Hock Keong* (Canton-Hokkien Temple). Both dialect groups are equally represented on the temple board, which served as a council and tribunal for the Chinese community in the early years of Penang.

In the 1880s, the Chinese Town Hall was formed to take over the economic and social functions of the Kong Hock Keong, which was left with the religious function. The Chinese Town Hall next door was rebuilt in the 1980s, and now dwarfs its mother temple.

Still the most popular Chinese temple.

PRANGIN LANE

In the vicinity of the Prangin Road Market is Prangin Lane and Fish Lane, which the Chinese call *Kiam Hu Thnia* (Salted Fish Yard). The area used to be marked by the strong smell of salted fish put out to sun.

FOOCHEW ASSOCIATION

The association of the Hakka dialect group from Foochew prefecture was founded in 1822 by Lee Hin, leader of the Ghee Hin secret society. Little is known about Lee Hin, except that he was a duck farmer and took a Malay wife.

Most of the stone-workers of early Penang were Foochews and their handiwork can still be seen in the carved granite columns of the association temple. They belonged to an as-sociation of stone-workers known as *Lean Seng Tong* (no longer extant) who laid the granite steps which lead to the Kek Lok Si and other temples in Ayer Itam, including the famous *Cheng Jee Chan* (One Thousand Two Hundred Steps) (see also Ayer Itam).

The building, which extended to Prangin Road, was renovated to its present form in 1905. In 1969, the Prangin Road section was redeveloped into a commercial building.

PRANGIN ROAD

Prangin River marked the limit of early 19th century George Town. The Chinese named the area *Sia Boey* (Town's End). The Prangin Canal is crossed by Anson Bridge at the end of Beach Street.

As the town consolidated, Prangin River became Prangin Creek, then Prangin Canal, then Prangin Ditch; by now it is no more than a large drain.

Early pictures show bullock carts parked along the canal, which was lined with tall casuarinas - hence the Malay place name *Pokok Rhu* (Casuarina Trees). If cleaned up and the banks replanted, the canal would offer a lovely promenade in the city centre.

THE PENANG HAIR-DRESSING & HAIR-WAVING ASSOCIATION

Barbers used to operate along the Prangin River by the junction of Sungai Ujong Road. Shorn hair was simply swept into the water. Among the barbers was Yeap Chor Ee, also known as *Theek Thau Ee,* who rose from rags to riches and eventually founded the Ban Hin Lee Bank (see also Beach Street).

Eng Seng Tong, an association of barbers, was founded in 1870 In this century, tradi-tional hair-dressing was transformed by the Western fashion of permanent hair-waving. Women moved into the male-dominated pro-fession and the trend spawned modern hair-dressing saloons with their typical Art Deco interiors. Many of Penang's "perm palours" still remain in this charming time warp.

Not to be left behind, the barber's associa-tion changed its name to Penang Hair-Dress-ing & Hair-Waving Association in 1953.

The Foochew Association with the granite columns carved by its own artisan members.

PRANGIN ROAD MARKET

The historic Prangin Road Market, housed in a 19th century market building, occupies both sides of the canal.

The wholesale market harks back to the days when fresh produce was brought by small boats up the Prangin River. The Tamils call it *Kala Kadai* or "morning market".

Some traditional food trades, such as preparing salted foodstuffs and making pastries, can still be found here. Food stalls open all night to cater to market workers.

The market association organises one of the largest Hungry Ghosts Festival celebration in town during the seventh lunar month (August-September).

SOO BENG DISPENSARY

Prangin Road has been renamed Jalan Dr. Lim Chwee Leong after the father of the former Chief Minister of Penang, Dr. Lim Chong Eu.

Chwee Leong was a historic personality in his own right. The distinguished medical practitioner and pediatrician was also President of Hu Yew Seah, the Straits Chinese British Association and the Chinese Recreation Club. He resided at *Su-Beng Hall* on Macalister Road.

Above right and left, the 19th century Prangin Market building with cast iron brackets. Middle right, the market straddling the Prangin Canal. Below, the Soo Beng Dispensary.

QUEEN STREET

The Malay street name *Gedung Rumput* or "Grass Godown" suggests that bullock carts were parked along this wide street.

The Chinese called this section *Chap Jee Keng Choo* (Twelve Houses) because there were originally a row of the same height.

A cohesive ensemble of Penang's early shophouses, from early to mid-19th century, can be seen at the northern end near Church Street. They are relatively squat and plain, their interiors are primitive, and some use rough logs instead of planed beams.

At the lower end of Queen Street there is a concentration of Indian petty traders. This is the location of the colourful *Ramadhan* market during fasting month, which sells a variety of festive Indian Muslim foods for breaking fast.

THE OPIUM AND SPIRIT FARM OFFICES

The "farms" were not fields for growing opium, but rather a system of government tenders which was applied to a variety of enterprises from gambling to tobacco.

The monopoly on opium and liqour allowed the colonial government to regulate the standards and "control" their distribution - privatized to the highest bidder, it also raised about half the total annual revenue of the Straits Settlements government.

The holders of the lucrative monopoly in turn farmed out licenses for the preparation and sale of opium to subcontractors who retailed the product at two to three times the cost of the raw Indian import. From these enormous profits, the "farmer" had to provide the preventive measures against smuggling and illegal distribution.

In 1907, the monopoly was contracted at 135,000 Straits Dollars a month, and sold

Originally an ensemble of twelve early shophouses of the same height; the Opium & Spirit Offices replaced six at the turn of the century, but the continuous arcade is retained.

through 145 licenced sub-farms in Penang and Province Wellesley.

The Penang Opium & Spirit Farm then consisted of the prominent members of the Straits Chinese society - the leading Hokkiens Cheah Chen Eok, Lim Kek Chuan and his son Lim Soo Chee, Lim Mah Chye, Lim Eow Hong, Yeoh Boon Chit, Yeoh Wee Gark, Khoo Cheow Teong, Ho Tiang Wan, Goh Boon Keng, Ong Hun Chong, and the leading Hakkas Leong Fee and Cheong Fatt Tze.

Members of the syndicate extended their prosperity through intermarriage - in an era when multiple wives and broods of children allowed ample opportunities for the elite families to be maritally united. Many of Penang's "old families" today are in fact related to them and to each other.

The Opium & Spirit Farm Offices, constructed in 1906 at a cost of 48,767 Straits Dollars were rented to the contractors for 900 Straits Dollars a month. It served as a godown and dispensary for *chandu,* or cooked opium, and *samsoo,* an alcohol distilled from rice and sugar. Opium was mainly consumed by the Chinese, and *samsoo* by the Indians.

But the modernisation of the Farm already marked the beginning of the end. That same year, the more progressive members of the Straits Chinese society started the Anti-Opium Movement, which gradually brought about the restriction and prohibition of the drug. Several other major social reform movements were similarly spearheaded in the first decade of the twentieth century.

The premises, now facing Pitt Street, are presently occupied by the offices and printing presses of *Star Publications.* The Star started in 1971 as a Penang newspaper and has grown into a national paper.

MAHAMARIAMMAN TEMPLE

The temple features the Hindu goddess Mariamman in her many incarnations. The complexity of Hindu mythology is reflected in the sculpture *(gopuram),* which is over 23 feet high and features 38 statues of gods and goddesses and four swans, over the entrance.

The site for a temple was granted to a chettiar in 1801 and the temple was built in 1833. It was renovated to its present form in its centenary year, with major works in 1978 executed by Madras sculptors.

During the Navarithri festival, the goddess Mariamman is taken out in a decorated wooden chariot which was donated by a pious Hindu woman in 1908.

The night procession tours *Little Madras,* the neighbourhood of Hindu shopkeepers and stevedores who are Mariamman's greatest devotees.

The Mahamariamman Temple during Thaipusam.

RESIDENCY ROAD

The road leading to the Residency was originally named "Race Course Road". It led in the other direction to the Race Course at the present St. George's Girls' School field.

Apart from the well-known Seri Mutiara, there was also the Mayor's Residence, which was sold to a private club during D.S. Ramanathan's term because it was deemed too extravagant for a Socialist Mayor. The Judge's Residence is on the adjoining Sepoy Lines Road.

In front of the Residency is the Polo Ground, formerly the Parade Ground, marched by the soldiers stationed at the military barracks along Sepoy Lines (see also Northam Lodge, Northam Road). Nearby are Barrack Road and the 19th century jail on Gaol Road.

THE SERI MUTIARA

The Residency, built in 1890 for the British Resident, is today the stately home of the Governor, Penang's Head of State. This grand residence, designed by a military engineer, was renovated on the occasion of its centenary. A manually-pulled Indian *punkah* still fans the Banquet Hall.

The mature grounds, through which meanders the Waterfall River, boast a collection of mature trees from all over the world, some of which are unique to the island.

GENERAL HOSPITAL

Officers from as far as India came to convalesce in Penang, which despite its malarial swamps was supposed to have had the healthiest climate in British India.

There was however no facility to look after the sick among the Asian poor until Mun Ah Foo started a private hospital for lepers and paupers. The Bengal-born Chinese who distinguished himself by wearing a black beaver hat was the leader of the Ghee Hin society from 1823 to 1858 (see also Rope Walk).

In 1854, he built the Pauper's Hospital at the junction of Residency and Hospital roads. A Mendicity Society and Coffin Fund was set up for the treatment of opium addicts, the impecunious and the homeless.

After his death, the Pauper's Hospital was managed by a committee of respectable community leaders headed by Lieutenant-Governor Anson himself. The Leper Hospital was relocated to Pulau Jerejak.

The colonial administration followed Ah Poo's initiative by building the General Hospital on an adjacent site. Constructed with convict labour in 1882, the General Hospital had European and Native wards, Male and Female Wards and a lunatic asylum.

In 1886, the Ghee Hin society donated the site of the Pauper's Hospital to the Municipality. The building was replaced with the Staff Nurses Hostel in 1930, while the General Hospital was rebuilt in 1935. Some old buildings from 1882 survived until 1990.

The former Mayor's Residency, now a private club.

ROPE WALK

The traditional method of making rope was to spin coconut husk fibres across many girders lined up along the street. Handcart-pullers and bullock-cart drivers gathered here to deliver the ropes to the waterfront where they were used for mooring ships.

In the latter half of the 19th century, many of these rope-spinners and cart-drivers joined the secret society called *Bendera Putih* (White Flag), which had its base at the *Mesjid Pintal Tali* (Rope Walk Mosque).

The White Flag, comprising Malays, Indians, Javanese and Boyanese, was led by Tuan Chee during the Penang Riots of 1867, when it teamed up with the Ghee Hin.

The White Flag became more respectable when it was boosted by the leadership of Syed Mashoor (d. 1922), who founded the Al-Mashoor School (see also Sheikh Al-Hadi's Residence, Jelutong Road).

At the turn of the century, the mosque congregation split up and half of them left to start the Prangin Road Mosque just at the nearby junction. The old mosque at Rope Walk was rebuilt in 1960.

Rope Walk kept its historic lumpen character with the daily thieves' market at the corner of Hong Kong Street, which survived until recently.

GHEE HIN HALL OF HEROES

Meng Eng Choo or "Memorial Hall of Heroes" was founded around 1890 to house the ancestral tablets of the Ghee Hin secret society leaders, including those who died in the Larut wars. The "Hall of Veterans", an association for old Ghee Hin members, occupies the upper floor.

The 19th century secret society comprised mainly the Chinese of the Teochew and Cantonese dialect groups. The working-class Cantonese in Penang were traditionally craftsmen, metalsmiths, plantation workers, fishermen and miners.

The Ghee Hin secret society, an offshoot of the Hung League in China, was one of the original triads in Penang. In the mid-19th century, their power in the Penang society was challenged by the locally-founded Khian Teik secret society and the Hai San secret society which derived from another stream of the Hung League.

The Ghee Hin-White Flag alliance in the end lost the territorial war in Penang to the Khian Teik-Red Flag alliance who were fewer

The doors guarding the Memorial Hall of Heroes.

Established in 1857, the temple has been renovated several times. Originally exclusive to a certain clan village in the Hokkien province, the association was opened to others of the same surname after the war.

The clan temple is situated in a court with an entrance from Beach Street which was formerly even narrower than it is today. It is surrounded by rowhouses of its own clan members and backs onto the Cheah Kongsi rowhouses on Toh Aka Lane.

Soo Hong Lane

The old Soo Hong Lane is the narrowest named street in George Town. Khoo Soo Hong, a landed proprietor and trader, was a founding senator on the Khoo Kongsi board in 1851.

in numbers but superior in arms and finances (see also Acheen Street and Armenian Street). As for Perak, the Ghee Hin were also given a raw deal in the Pangkor engagement (see also Pangkor Road).

In the end, the victors rose to social respectability, while the losers sank to obscurity. Around 1890, the Hai San took over the Ghee Hin base in Church Street, and the latter moved into Rope Walk, right next to the mosque of their Muslim allies (see also Church Street).

Seh Tan Court

"The Tans and Lims cover the mountains and the seas", goes a popular saying about the two most common surnames in Penang.

Above, Rope Walk today. Below, Soo Hong Lane.

STEWART LANE

The Stewarts are a well-known Penang Eurasian family who once lived down this street (see also Love Lane).

The narrowest unnamed street in town with houses on both sides lies off Stewart Lane. It has no official name, but is locally called *Sampan Hang* (Boat Alley). Its original inhabitants were former Lee clan jetty members who worked as Channel ferrymen.

SRI BAHARI ROAD

A North Indian temple was first established by Hindu members of the Bengali Regiment of the East India Company.

In 1833, the Sri Kunj Bihari Temple in Penang Road was endowed by Hindus from

Above, a mansion tucked away on Stewart Lane. Below, possibly a former Eurasian home.

Bihar, North India. This community, traditionally comprising dairy farmers and cooks, has dwindled in numbers in this century.

The endowment includes the houses on Sri Bahari Road, which should probably have been named Sri *Bihari* Road.

The temple was little known until after the war, when the late Shri D. S. Joshi, a Gujerati merchant, became chairman of the temple and promoted it to other groups of the North Indian Hindu community.

Today, the temple, popularly known as *Thakorwadi,* is the religious centre for the Gujerati, Sindhi, Bengali and Punjabi minorities of Hindu faith.

TANJONG TOKONG ROAD

Tanjung Tokong is an old fishing village and probably the earliest Chinese village on the island. The Tua Pek Kong Temple has been there from the beginning, as evidenced by the local Malay name *Tanjung Tokong* (Cape of the Temple).

The position of the temple is so geomantically significant that the Hokkien and Hakka dialect groups have disputed claims to the site for two centuries.

There are also two Tua Pek Kong temples in town - the Armenian Street Tua Pek Kong Temple for the Hokkien community and the King Street Tua Pek Kong Temple for the Hakka and Cantonese community, each dialect group jealously guarding its own patron of prosperity. Each town temple organises its own procession to the mother temple in Tanjong Tokong, on the full moon nights of Chinese New Year.

Tanjung Tokong was a popular seaside resort in prewar days. There is an abandoned lookout, seating areas among the rocks and a small public pavilion sponsored by Aw Boon Haw of *Tiger Balm* fame. Today the open-air crab-eating restaurant is still a nostalgic spot for locals.

The Tua Pek Kong Temple and the burial mound next to it.

TUA PEK KONG TEMPLE

The Sea Pearl Temple is dedicated to the *Tua Pek Kong* - literally, "Great-Grand Uncle", symbolically, the "Protector of the Land". He is more commonly regarded as the God of Prosperity.

On the 14th night of the Chinese New Year, the Poh Hock Seah stages the *Chneah Hoay* (Flame-Watching Ceremony) ritual here (see also the Hokkien Tua Pek Kong Temple, Armenian Street). Embers in a ceremonial urn are fanned until the flames leap up, and the coming year's fortune is divined in this conflagration.

Many Chinese settlements in the Nanyang have their own *Tua Pek Kong* - Penang's deified pilgrim father is Chang Li, a Hakka scholar and an exile from 18th century China.

According to the Hakka legend, he settled in Penang before the arrival of Francis Light. He had come here with two brothers, the last of whom died in 1796, and all three are buried on the mound beside the temple.

The story that Chang Li was a teacher, and his two brothers, a brick-maker and a metalsmith, could be apocryphal. Among them - one could teach, the second could build houses, the third could make weapons - these three pilgrim fathers would have had all the skills required to build a new society.

TOH AKA LANE

An old ironsmith's shop survives from the street called *Phak Theek Kay Hang-Ah* or "Ironsmith's Alley".

An unexpected sight along this narrow street is the Penang Eng Tai Hoay Kuan, an association of the Hakka dialect groups of Eng Teng and Tai Pu districts, founded in 1840.

Tok Aka Lane runs into the back lane of the Acheen Street Mosque. The section which connects with Malay Street has a row of houses with painted panels under the eaves. The well-maintained clan rowhouses belong to the Cheah Kongsi, and many Cheah families still live there.

Below, cornices decorated by an early artist. Above, the facade is maintained with all its original elements.

TRANSFER ROAD

Transfer Road commemorates the transfer of the Straits Settlements government from the Indian Office to the Colonial Office in Singapore in 1867.

The much-celebrated Transfer meant "direct rule" for the Straits Settlements, which resulted in a more efficient administration and an era of great prosperity for the Crown colonies.

The canal from the Prangin River was joined to a "bound ditch" at Transfer Road, which spilled into the sea at the North Beach. Small boats used to come up to the site of the Keramat Dato Koya.

In the 19th century, the urban Jawi Peranakan communities were found along the main arterial roads - east of Penang Road and at the town end of Burma Road, Macalister Road and Dato Kramat Road.

Today, many pockets of these fine Indo-Malay houses survive along Transfer Road and its side streets - Halfway Road Ariffin Road, Dindings Road, Hutton Lane and Kedah Road (see also Kedah Road).

In the early 20th century, the majority of the Jawi Peranakan moved out, and the neighbourhood was taken over by Tamil Muslims from Kadaiyanallur.

KERAMAT DATO KOYA

Dato Koya, alias Syed Mustapha Idris, came to Penang from Malabar, fleeing arrest for a murder he did not commit. He became a saint among the convict labourers, whom he supernaturally protected from unjust treatment. He was a miracle worker who healed the sick and fed the masses.

When he died in 1840, Dato Koya's followers in the public works built his tomb and shrine on the spot where he used to sit under the trees. The authorities not only granted the land but also named the nearby road Dato Koya Road.

The original followers of Dato Koya were the Malabaris who lived in Kampung Malabar and Dato Koya Road.

Today, the *roti canai* shops next to the Keramat Dato Koya serve a good breakfast. The Indian bread-sellers on bicycles collect their loaves from the Ismalia Bakery across the street.

UNITED MUSLIM ASSOCIATION

The largest group of Tamil Muslims in Penang today (estimated to be twenty thousand) originate from one small village in India known as Kadaiyanallur in Tirunalveli district, South India.

Kadaiyanallur was a weaving village which faced massive unemployment at the beginning of the industrial revolution when cotton goods began to be manufactured in England.

In the late 19th century, they emigrated through the port of Negapatam to Penang in large numbers. In the early 20th century, the womenfolk also came along and until after the Second World War, the Kadaiyanallur immigrants did not marry outside their group.

The mausoleum of the saint of convict workers.

Tunku Kudin was appointed Viceroy *(Wakil Yam Tuan)* of Selangor by his father-in-law, to arbitrate the disputes between Raja Abdullah and Raja Mahdi. The two contended to be chief of Selangor, a position which entailed the right to collect duty at Klang and Kuala Selangor on the tin that was mined upstream.

In 1929, the United Muslim Association was formed to unite various social groups from Kadaiyanallur who had taken up residence in Penang. The first chairman was A.K. Abdulrahman, a veterinary worker in the Municipal Council abattoirs.

Before the war, only one son of the community had the opportunity to sit for the Senior Cambridge Examinations. Realising that their children were deprived of a proper education, the association members started a vernacular school, which then became the state-run Sekolah Rendah Kebangsaan Tamil (since discontinued).

Another two Kadaiyanallur associations are found on Kedah Road and Chulia Street.

As in Perak, the Chinese tin-miners in Selangor were also divided between the Ghee Hin and Hai San secret societies (see also Pangkor Road).

Tunku Kudin took the side of Raja Abdullah, and was supported by Yap Ah Loy, chief of the Hai San tin-miners as well as Kapitan China of Kuala Lumpur.

Raja Mahdi was allied to the Selangor aristocracy who resented interference by the Kedah prince, and their confederates were the Ghee Hin tin-miners.

The civil war lasted for seven years until 1874, when Selangor came under the protection of the British. The latter continued to recognize Tengku Kudin as Viceroy.

UDINI ROAD

Udini Road and the adjacent Tengku Kudin Road are named after Tunku Dhiauddin ibni Almarhum Sultan Zainul Rashid. As crown prince *(Raja Muda)* of Kedah, he married the daughter of the Sultan of Selangor.

TUNKU KUDIN HOUSE

After matters were resolved in Selangor, Tunku Kudin was informed that his brother the Sultan of Kedah had banned him from his own state and appointed another as Crown Prince.

Tunku Kudin was accused of being a traitor to the Malays, befriending foreigners and interfering in the affairs of another state.

The United Muslim Association, housed in a traditional Peranakan Jawi bungalow which was acquired by the association before the war, now demolished.

His residence at Bukit Tinggi, Alor Setar, was confiscated.

Tunku Kudin bided his time in Penang, staying at the house on Northam Road next to the *Istana Kedah* (see also Northam Road). When the Kedah Sultan died in 1778, Tunku Kudin tried to persuade the King of Siam to recognize his candidate for the succession, but failed.

After 1882, when it became increasingly clear that his political enemies, led by the aristocrat Wan Mat Saman, would continue to hold sway in Kedah, Tunku Kudin decided to retire permanently in Penang.

Tunku Kudin's mansion occupies a breath-taking hilltop site, overlooking the Channel. In the grounds was an aviary and free-roaming deer. The prince of Kedah took his evening rides around the hill in a horse-drawn carriage.

Until his death in 1906, Tunku Kudin alternated between his two residences in Penang, making occasional outstation trips to Selangor. The property was later acquired by the British. It has served as a Japanese naval base, British government quarters, an RAAF base and was more recently used by the Marine Police.

Tunku Kudin was the grand-uncle of the late Tunku Abdul Rahman (see also Ayer Rajah Road), a Kedah prince who became the first Prime Minister of Malaysia. The Tunku related the story that a delegation of Penang actors and theatre promoters approached Tunku Kudin, asking him to name their new theatre form. It was a Malay version of the Indian musical drama *Indera Saba.*

Tunku Kudin pondered the matter and finally decided that since it was a make-believe drama, it should be called *Bangsawan* (literally "nobility"), as all *"wans"* were play-actors and simulators.

The name given by Tunku Kudin, which was meant as a slight upon his archrival Wan Mat Saman, has endured in the history of Malay theatre (see also Aboo Siti Lane).

Tengku Kudin's Mansion on his very own hill, currently still derelict.

intervention of amateur novelist Ishikawa Tatsuzo, Chief of the Japanese Military Propaganda Bureau, who had a four-sided signboard of the Broadcasting Station erected on the pedestal to conceal the statue.

To avoid suspicion, the signboard was topped with a Nippon flag, and the four British lions at the pedestal base were made to bear the emblems of the Rising Sun in place of their Union Jacks.

VICTORIA STREET

BOON SAN TONG KHOO KONGSI

The lesser known Khoo Kongsi was built by a branch of the Leong San Tong Khoo clan. Khoo Thean Teik, who belonged to this branch, made it the most powerful component group of the Khoo clan during his lifetime (see also Cannon Square). He was a main founder of the temple in 1878.

The original entrance was via a narrow passageway from Beach Street, directly opposite Seh Tan Court. The sea-facing temple was renovated in 1907, and its entrance changed to the then newly created Victoria Street. The work was done just a year after the Khoo Kongsi at Cannon Square, and probably by the same craftsmen.

VICTORIA GREEN ROAD

CHINESE RECREATION CLUB

In the days when the European and Eurasian communities each had their sporting clubs, the Straits Chinese resolved to have one of their own. The Club was founded principally for playing football in 1892. Cricket, hockey and rugby were played; soccer and tennis champions were produced.

The present building was erected in the early 1930s on a playing field called Victoria Green. At one corner stands the Queen Victoria Memorial erected by those who considered themselves "the Queen's Chinese". The statue was unveiled by the Governor of the Straits Settlements in 1930, some three decades after the death of Her Majesty.

During the Second World War, the Club was used as the Broadcasting Station of the Japanese Occupation Army.

Queen Victoria's statue would have been melted down for making bullets, if not for the

Above left, the very late Victorian statue. Below, the Boon San Tong Khoo Kongsi.

WATERFALL ROAD

The earliest form of tourism in Penang was eco-tourism. European travellers who stopped in Penang between India and China came to see the Great Waterfall, hence Waterfall Road was one of the earliest interior roads, already extant in 1800.

The dramatic waterfall which cascades over 400 feet and flows into the Waterfall Garden was also the subject of many early paintings. It was considered a "Lion" or a "Monster" attraction. Here, the travellers bathed and rested in an oasis of lush greenery - a most refreshing experience after weeks at sea.

A tourist to Penang in the early 19th century, Ibrahim Munshi (son of well-known Abdullah Munshi) made the compulsory visit to the "Waterfall Garden", which he records in his *Kisah Pelayaran:*

... we stopped at a hotel which is a resting place for people who come to bathe in the pool at the foot of the hill. There were people all over the place; the bathing place was divided into three classes and the charges were according to the classes; other amenities were also available there e.g. food, drink and game of billiards; charges were reasonable. There were also changing rooms. The water springs from the hill, clear and cool, it flows down in torrents in the same volume between rocks and boulders. The ponds are constructed with stones.

At the turn of the century, the E & O Hotel advertised a visit to the Crag Hotel - 45-minutes by rickshaw to the *Alexandria Baths* at Waterfall Road, and another 45 minutes by sedan chair, carried by coolies. Modern transport has not shortened travelling time.

In 1910, after the Penang Botanic Gardens was established, the water authorities considered creating a reservoir by blocking off the entrance of the garden and flooding the valley. Fortunately, only a small reservoir was eventually built and the gardens were saved, but the waterfall has since been inaccessible to the public.

PENANG BOTANIC GARDENS

When created in 1884, the Penang Botanic Gardens incorporated the existing Waterfall Garden and the nearby granite quarry which had enlarged the natural valley over the years.

The Penang Botanic Gardens was founded as "a nursery for the planting of colonial products". From the nursery, Charles Curtis, founder and first Superintendent of the Gardens, planted many of Penang's roadside trees.

The Waterfall - not as voluminous as in former times.

humid forests. The Lower Circular Road takes one past two prominent groups of palms and distinctive bamboos clusters along the Waterfall River that flows through the gardens. A shady jungle path leads to the romantic Lily Pond.

Two orchid houses provide comparison between cultivated hybrids and wild orchid species. The best time to admire the flowering trees is during the dry season, from February to April, when the Thai Bungor (*Lagestroemia Loudonii*), the Javanese Cassia (*Cassia javanica*) and the Rosy trumpet (*Tabebuia rosea*) burst in glorious sprays of colour.

The gardens has two band stands. The covered metal and concrete structure built after the war is occasionally used by school brass bands. The original bandstand consists only of a cleanly-shaped grass mound, as it was the policy of the gardens to rely on

An apt tribute to Curtis' memory is the tree called *Shorea curtisii*. The Shorea is easily spotted in the surrounding hills as its silver foliage glitters in the sunlight.

Economic and horticultural plants were regularly introduced from the Kew Gardens to the Singapore Botanic Gardens, and thereafter to the Penang Botanic Gardens. During the Straits Settlements days, the Botanic Gardens of Penang and Singapore came under the same Director. One of them, the late Prof. R.E. Holttum, Director from 1927 to 1941, wrote many authoritative books on Malayan plants. The staghorn fern, named *Platycerium holtumii* after him, still flourishes in the Penang Botanic Gardens' Fern House.

To the botanist, the amateur gardener and the plant-lover, the 72-acre gardens are a never-ending source of pleasure. Here one finds exotic plants like gingers, anturiums, and monkey cups in the dark,

Above, the natural valley. Below, the monkeys.

natural landscaping as much as possible. The formal garden, with small flowering plants along an aisle leading to an old pavilion, is similarly understated.

During the Second World War, a famous drinking party of Japanese and German officers was held on the expansive lawn between the mound and the running stream. The strategic site of the sheltered valley with a supply of fresh water was not missed by the Japanese navy, who used the Botanic Gardens as one of their bases in Penang. A few reminders of the Occupation still survive.

A site near the Lily Pond, where once stood a torpedo assembly shed, is still currently referred to as "Torpedo". Explosives were hidden in nearby tunnels dug into the hills, and it is recounted that a few of the local men recruited to dig these tunnels were buried alive.

A great attraction is the monkeys which used to come down in hordes from the surrounding hill forests. They are the Long-Tailed Macaque *(Macaca fascicularis),* native to the island. Since feeding was discouraged by the authorities, they have become less evident in the gardens.

It takes about fifteen minutes to walk briskly around the Lower Circular Road, and another twenty minutes if you want to explore the Upper Circular Road and the Upper North Road.

There are various hiking paths from the Botanic Gardens to the famous Penang Hill. The most popular among joggers and walkers is the Jeep Track, a tarred road which begins right next to the gardens' entrance. This was the historic path by which European travellers proceeded on sedan chair or Acehnese ponies.

The former social segregation on Penang hill started at the bottom, and Asians took the natural hiking trail from the old Moon Gate, several hundred metres down the road.

The Formal Garden.

DEWAN MAHATMA GANDHI

One of the active organisers of the Thaipusam festival is the *Hindu Mahajana Sangam,* an association of waterfront workers formed in 1935. The association looked after the workers' welfare and later developed a labour union (see also Weld Quay).

The "rest and festive house", renamed in 1948 after Mahatma Gandhi's assassination, is used for religious retreat and also to accommodate outstation estate workers who come to Penang for the festivals.

WATERFALL HILLTOP TEMPLE

The convict labourers who built Farquhar's aqueduct erected a Hindu shrine by the waterfall, depicted in Cazalet's watercolour of 1856. This was apparently the original destination of the annual Thaipusam procession (see also Farquhar Street).

When the waterfall was closed off to the public in 1904, the Hindu shrine had to be removed. The lance *(vel)* representing Murugan was lodged so firmly in the ground it could not be pulled out and had to be snapped off. It was reconsecrated at the Waterfall Hilltop Temple.

Befitting the hill setting, the temple is called *Balathendayuthapani,* as it is dedicated to the young incarnation of Murugan retreating in the hills.

The waterfall foothills have always been sacred to the Hindus; they call this area *Thanner Malai* (Water Hill).

Above, the Waterfall Hilltop Temple during Thiru Karthigei. Below, the 19th century building now called the Dewan Mahatma Gandhi.

Murugan) consecrated in 1857. The building, laid out according to a *chokkatan* (chequered) design, is of fine crafts-manship and decoration. The complex, surrounded by a walled compound, has been well-preserved. Behind is a kitchen with large pots for mass feed-ing during festival times.

On Thaipusam eve, the male chettiar carry the peacock feather yoke, accompanying the silver chariot along Waterfall Road. They retreat to the *chettinar* for three days before accompanying the chariot back.

Behind the Chettiar temple is a large Indian village on Mount Erskine Hill which once supplied the labour for sedan chair transport up to Penang Hill, before the hill railway was built. The village was then called *Nakali Thandal,* or "Sedan Mandur", after the supervisor of the sedan-carriers.

NATTUKKOTTAI CHETTIAR TEMPLE

In 1854, shortly after the chettiar commu-nity established themselves in Penang Street, they purchased the land in Waterfall Road to build a *chettinar,* or chettiar quarters (see also Koil Vidhu, Penang Street).

Within the *chettinar* is a temple dedicated to *Thendayuthapani* (an incarnation of

Above, the chettinar. Below left, part of the temple complex. Below right, the finely-decorated temple aisles, the floor covered with rice flour drawings during festival time.

WELD QUAY

Since Penang lost its free port status in 1974, Penang's waterfront has sadly declined into a backwater. The seat of government shifted from Downing Street to Komtar, changing the whole orientation of the city. George Town now tends to look inland rather than toward the sea.

Occasionally military ships and glamorous cruise vessels that dock at Swettenham Pier remind the locals of the glorious port that Penang once was.

The cluttered but still picturesque waterfront can best be seen when George Town is approached by ferry. The ferries, purchased from Hong Kong, carry both passengers and vehicles between the Pengkalan Tun Uda Ferry Terminal in George Town and Butterworth on the mainland.

The Church Street Ghaut Pier formerly used by cars boarding the Ferry Steamers, is now only used by small boats.

There were formerly two more jetties before the war - the Railway Jetty at China Street Ghaut and the Victoria Pier at Downing Street Ghaut (see also China Street Ghaut). Ocean steamers either tied up alongside the Swettenham Pier, or anchored in the roads; in the latter case, passengers would take the launch service to the Victoria Pier, where they would be met by "hotel runners".

Weld Quay was created during the 1880s when Frederick Aloysius Weld was Governor of the Straits Settlements. The massive land reclamation project culminated in the development of Swettenham Pier which, when completed in 1904, boosted Penang to a modern transshipment centre. The government goods sheds were added in 1907 for lease to shipping agents.

The Indians called Weld Quay *Kitengi Teru* (Street of Company Godowns). The

Above, the Boustead block of trading houses, now hardly visible from the sea.

godowns are still used by Indian stevedores transporting rope with hand-pulled carts.

In the days when shipping was a highly labour intensive activity, two Tamil Muslim clans, the Maraicar and the Rawther, were the main contractors for both Hindu and Muslim Indian coolies.

Weld Quay was the birthplace of *Kelinga Mee,* a hybrid of Chinese fried noodles and an Indian-style seafood fritter salad (*Pasembur*). Now a famous Penang hawker dish, *Kelinga Mee* was originally created for the appetites of sailors and port workers along Weld Quay.

PATERSON SIMONS GODOWNS

The free-standing building was developed in the 1890s by Phuah Hin Leong and then rented to Paterson Simons (see also Phuah Hin Leong Road). A picturesque alley paved with granite ballasts leads to the godowns.

Opposite page, from left, Wisma Yeap Chor Ee, Malayan Railway building (Wisma Kastam), the former Paterson Simons building and the former North Borneo building. Below, alley through the Paterson Simons Godowns.

BOUSTEAD BLOCK

Boustead, which constructed the first of these buildings on newly reclaimed land in 1893, is still based there today. The company used to refine and export tin ingots with the Boustead trademark.

The ensemble of shipping offices and godowns extends all the way to Beach Street. Down the row were other European merchant houses like Schmidt & Kuesterman, Behn Meyer and Shiffman Heer which all began as branches of the Singapore offices.

CLAN JETTIES

In the 19th century, dragon boat races were held in the North Channel by Penang's historic clan jetties. This tradition was more recently revived as competitive sports events for the Pesta Pulau Pinang in the 1950s.

There were originally seven "clan jetties"; these were in fact clan villages built over the water. The Ong Jetty was dismantled when the Ferry Terminal was built. Six remain - from north to south, they are the Lim Jetty, Chew Jetty, Tan Jetty, Yeoh Jetty, Lee Jetty,

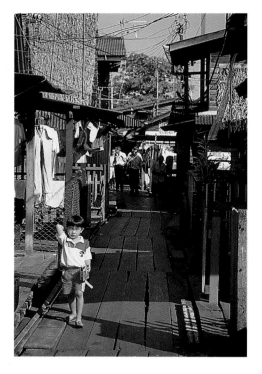

Koay Jetty; the seventh is the "assorted surname jetty".

The jetty with the largest community is the Chew Jetty near Armenian Street Ghaut.

The Chew stevedores supply fresh water to the ships.

The end of the Chew Jetty is the mooring place for Burmese trawlers which bring rubber, timber and other materials from Burma. The sturdily-built, deeply-tanned men in checked sarungs who hang around the jetty are unmistakably Burmese sailors.

Above, the wooden plank walkway of Chew Jetty, lined with attap-roofed houses on stilts. Below, the stevedore station at the end of Chew Jetty. Behind is the mooring place of Burmese boats.

MASONIC TEMPLE

Many of the leading members of the European community in the Straits Settlements were Freemasons.

The Penang Lodges had names like Lodge Royal Prince of Wales, Victoria Jubilee Chapter, Gottlieb Mark Lodge and Scotia Chapter.

A prominent mason was Felix Henry Gottlieb (after whom Gottlieb Road was named), initiated in 1850.

The Freemason's Society was exempted from the Societies Ordinance of 1890, which banned all other secret societies. Today, the Lodges are still active and include Asian members.

WESTERN ROAD

At the turn of the century, the Europeans moved away from the old suburbs of Northam Road and Anson Road, which were being colonised by the Chinese elite, and out into the countryside around the Residency and the sporting clubs.

The Westerners transformed the area around Western Road into a country suburb comprising York Road, Scotland Road, Residency Road and part of Macalister Road.

THE WESTERN ROAD CEMETERY

Christian burials after the late 19th century took place at the Western Road cemetery.

Here are the graves of Huttenbach, Arshak Sarkies, an Armenian mass grave, and a Russian memorial to those who sank with the *Zemschug* during the First World War (see also Jelutong Road, Farquhar Street, Armenian Street and Esplanade for respective mentions).

PENANG SPORTS CLUB

This elite sporting club was founded in 1900 for playing tennis, bowls and golf. In 1939, it took over a 19th century building on this site, formerly the Military Hospital. The club house was renovated in 1992.

Above, the Masonic Lodge. Below, the Zemschug memorial.

YAHUDI ROAD

JEWISH CEMETERY

Penang had a small community of Jews whom the locals called *orang Yahudi*. Like the Armenians, they came from India along the trade route. The Jewish Cemetery, which has over a hundred graves from the 19th and early 20th centuries, is well maintained.

YORK ROAD

The old character of George Town's country roads can be seen in York Road, lined with giant Angsana trees. York Road was once "The Road to Scotland" referring to James Scott's estate, (hence Scotland Road) which lay at the foothills of Batu Gantong.

YORK ROAD MOSQUE

This mosque is charmingly set in a walled compound along the Waterfall River. The main benefactor in 1914 was Sheikh Ghani, Penang's first Muslim harbour pilot, who also founded the Pahang Road Mosque (see also Burmah Road).

Above, the Jewish cemetery. Below, the York Road Mosque.

Lo Man Yuk, *Chinese Names of Streets in Penang.* **Journal of the Singapore Branch of the Royal Asiatic Society (JSBRAS), 1900: 33, 197-246.** Chinese street names at the turn of the century.

Durai Raja Singham S., *Malayan Street Names.* **Ipoh.** Contains over seventy street names in Penang, including many of colonial origin.

Purcell, Victor, *Early Penang,* **1896-1928.** Penang: Pinang Gazette Press, 1928. 141 pg. Contains a map from 1807 and a short account of the development of the streets at the time.

Stevens, F.G., *A Contribution to the Early History of Prince of Wales Island.* **Journal of the Malayan Branch of the Royal Asiatic Society (JMBRAS), 1929: 7, 377-414.** George Town's early development traced in detail, with some analysis of land ownership, use, administration and planning.

Wright, Arnold & Cartwright, H.A. (ed.), *Twentieth Century Impressions of British Malaya: Its History, People, Commerce, Industries and Resources.* **London: Lloyd's Greater Britain Pub. Co. 1908. 3 vol.** Rare book. The chapter on Penang, illustrated with black-and-white photographs of historic buildings, interiors and personalities, gives a rich impression of Penang society at that time.

Historical Personalities of Penang, The Historical Personalities of Penang Committee, 1986, 180 pages. Features over 150 personalities of Penang society.

Lim Chong Keat, *Penang Views, 1770-1860,* Penang Museum, Summer Times Publishing, 1986, 236 pages. Over 160 paintings, drawings and prints reproduced with commentaries.

Penang, Past & Present, 1786-1963. The City Council of George Town, Penang, 1966, 128 pg. The evolution of the local government and the issues which concerned the town administration.

Tan Poh Choo, Joceline, *History of Penang: A Selected and Annotated Bibliography,* Kumpulan Wang Majlis Perbandaran Pulau Pinang untuk Pengajian Pembangunan, dan Perpustakaan Universiti Sains Malaysia, Pulau Pinang, 1991, 170 pages. Contains over 700 entries of published and unpublished accounts, as well as a list of newspapers and periodicals and administrative records.

Wooden manholes are still found on Church Street and Penang Street.

Demolished.

STREET INDEX

The following is a selection of old street names (left column) and their contemporary names (corresponding right column).

A

Aboo Siti Lane	Lorong Abu Siti
Acheen Street	Lebuh Acheh
Adams Road	Jalan Adams
Ah Quee Street	Lebuh Ah Quee
Amoy Lane	Lorong Amoy
Anson Road	Jalan Anson
Argus Lane	Lorong Argus
Argyll Road	Jalan Argyll
Ariff Crescent	Lengkok Ariff
Ariffin Court	Halaman Ariffin
Ariffin Road	Jalan Ariffin
Armenian Street	Lebuh Armenian
Arratoon Road	Jalan Arratoon
Ayer Itam Road	Jalan Ayer Itam
Ayer Puteh Road	Jalan Ayer Puteh
Ayer Rajah Road	Jalan Tunku Abdul Rahman

B

Babington Avenue	Lebuhraya Babington
Bagan Jermal Road	Jalan Bagan Jermal
Bakau Street	Lebuh Bakau
Balik Pulau Road	Jalan Balik Pulau
Bangkok Lane	Lorong Bangkok
Barnett Road	Jalan Barnett
Barrack Road	Jalan Barrack
Batu Gantong Road	Jalan Batu Gantong
Batu Lanchang Road	Jalan Batu Lanchang
Bawasah Road	Jalan Bawasah
Beach Street	Lebuh Pantai
Bell Road	Jalan Bell
Bertam Lane	Lorong Bertam
Bidor Lane	Lorong Bidor
Biggs Road	Jalan Biggs
Bingham Avenue	Lebuhraya Bingham
Birch Road	Jalan Birch
Bishop Street	Lebuh Bishop
Bodhi Avenue	Lebuhraya Bodhi
Boundary Road	Jalan Boundary
Brick Kiln Road	Jalan Brick Kiln
Bridge Street	Jalan C.Y. Choy
Brook Road	Jalan Brook
Brown Road	Jalan Brown
Brunei Lane	Lorong Brunei
Buckingham Street	Lebuh Buckingham
Burmah Road	Jalan Burma

C

Camp Road	Jalan Camp
Campbell Street	Lebuh Campbell
Calthrope Road	Jalan Calthrope
Cannon Square	Medan Cannon
Cannon Street	Lebuh Cannon
Cantonment Road	Jalan Cantonment
Carnarvon Street	Lebuh Carnarvon
Caunter Hall Road	Jalan P. Ramlee
Cecil Street	Lebuh Cecil
Ceylon Lane	Lorong Ceylon
Cheah Choo Yew Road	Jalan Cheah Choo Yew
Cheapside	Cheapside
Che Em Lane	Lorong Che Em
Che Rose Road	Jalan Che' Rose
Cheeseman Road	Jalan Cheeseman
Chetty Lane	Lorong Ceti
China Street	Lebuh China
China Street Ghaut	Gat Lebuh China
Chin Ho Square	Medan Chin Ho
Chow Thye Road	Jalan Chow Thye
Chowrasta Road	Jalan Chowrasta
Chulia Street	Lebuh Chulia

Church Street	Lebuh Gereja
Cintra Street	Lebuh Cintra
Claimant Place	Pesara Claimant
Clarke Street	Lebuh Clarke
Clove Hall Road	Jalan Clove Hall
Codrington Avenue	Lebuhraya Codrington
College Lane	Pesiaran College
College Square	Medan Maktab
Concordia Road	Jalan Concordia
Cross Street	Lebuh Lintang

D

Dato Koyah Road	Jalan Dato Koya
Dato Kramat Road	Jalan Dato Kramat
David Chen Gardens	Taman David Chen
Dickens Street	Lebuh Dickens
Dindings Road	Jalan Dindings
Downing Street	Lebuh Downing
Drury Lane	Lorong Drury
Duke Street	Lebuh Duke
Dundas Court	Dundas Court
Dunlop Road	Jalan Dunlop
Dunn Road	Jalan Dunn

E

East Avenue	East Avenue
Edgecumbe Road	Jalan Edgecumbe
Esplanade Road	Jalan Padang Kota Lama
Evergreen Road	Jalan Evergreen

F

Faraday Road	Jalan Faraday
Farquhar Street	Lebuh Farquhar
Fettes Road	Jalan Fettes
Fish Lane	Lorong Ikan
Fort Road	Jalan Tun Syed Sheh Barakbah
Free School Road	Jalan Free School

G

Glugor Road	Jalan Sultan Azlan Shah
Gaol Road	Jalan Gaol
Gladstone Road	Jalan Gladstone
Gopeng Road	Jalan Gopeng
Gottlieb Road	Jalan Gottlieb
Green Hall	Green Hall
Green Lane	Jalan Masjid Negeri
Grove Road	Jalan Grove
Gurney Drive	Pesiaran Gurney

H

Hala Sungei Pinang	Hala Sungai Pinang
Halfway Road	Lorong Sekerat
Hamilton Road	Jalan Hamilton
Happy Valley Road	Jalan Lembah Ria
Hargreaves Road	Jalan Hargreaves
Herriot Street	Lebuh Herriot
Hilir Sungei Pinang	Hilir Sungai Pinang
Hill Railway Station Road	Jalan Stesen Keretapi Bukit
Hock Hin Terrace	Tingkat Hock Hin
Hogan Road	Jalan Hogan
Hongkong Street	Jalan Cheong Fat Tze
Hospital Road	Jalan Hospital
Ho Tiang Wan Road	Jalan Ho Tiang Wan
Hutchings Garden	Taman Hutchings
Hutton Lane	Jalan Hutton

I

Ibbetson Road	Jalan Ibbetson
Immigration Road	Jalan Imigresen
Ipoh Lane	Lorong Ipoh
Irrawaddy Road	Jalan Irrawaddi
Irving Road	Jalan Irving

J

Jalan Abdullah Ariff	Jalan Abdullah Ariff
Jalan Ahmad bin Abdul Rahman	Jalan Maqbul
Jalan Batu Jantan	Jalan Batu Jantan
Jalan Batu Perempuan	Jalan Batu Perempuan
Jalan Brother James	Jalan Brother James
Jalan Bukit Dambar	Jalan Bukit Dumbar
Jalan Bukit Gambir	Jalan Bukit Gambiar
Jalan Bukit Glugor	Jalan Bukit Gelugor
Jalan Bukom	Jalan Bukom
Jalan Deva Pada	Jalan Deva Pada
Jalan Dharma	Jalan Dharma
Jalan Gajah	Jalan Gajah
Jalan Haji Ahmad	Jalan Haji Ahmad
Jalan Haji Hashim Imam	Jalan Haji Hashim Imam
Jalan Hajjah Remah	Jalan Hajjah Rehmah
Jalan Helen Brown	Jalan Helen Brown
Jalan Kampong Custom	Jalan Kampong Kastam
Jalan Kampong Melayu	Jalan Kampong Melayu
Jalan Kampong Pisang	Jalan Kampong Pisang
Jalan Kampong Rawa	Jalan Kampong Rawa
Jalan Kota Giam	Jalan Kota Giam
Jalan Madrasah	Jalan Madrasah
Jalan Mohd. Taib	Jalan Md. Taib
Jalan Mohd. Khan	Jalan Mohd. Khan
Jalan Oldham	Jalan Oldham
Jalan Ong Joo Sun	Jalan Ong Joo Sun
Jalan Osman bin Kadir Lit	Jalan Osman bin Kadir Lit
Jalan Singapura	Jalan Singapura
Jalan Sir Hussein	Jalan Sir Husein
Jalan Sir Ibrahim	Jalan Sir Ibrahim
Jalan Sungei Kelian	Jalan Sungai Kelian
Jalan Sungkai	Jalan Sungkai
Jalan Talipon	Jalan Telefon
Jalan Ria	Jalan Ria
Jelutong Road	Jalan Jelutong
Jesselton Road	Jalan Jesselton
Jockey Road	Jalan Joki
Jalan Johore	Jalan Johor
Jones Road	Jalan Jones
Juru Lane	Lorong Juru

K

Kajang Road	Jalan Kajang
Kampar Road	Jalan Kampar
Kampong Bharu	Kampung Baru
Kampong Deli	Kampong Deli
Kampong Dodol	Jalan Kampong Dodol
Kampong Java Bharu	Kampong Jawa Baru
Kampong Java Lama	Kampong Jawa Lama
Kampong Kaka	Kampong Kaka
Kampong Kolam	Kampong Kolam
Kampong Malabar	Jalan Kampong Malabar
Katz Street	Lebuh Katz
Kebun Nyor Road	Jalan Kebun Nyor
Kedah Road	Jalan Kedah
Kek Chuan Road	Jalan Kek Chuan
Kelantan Road	Jalan Kelantan
Kelawei Road	Jalan Kelawai
Keng Kwee Street	Lebuh Keng Kwee
Kennedy Road	Jalan Kennedy
Khaw Sim Bee Road	Jalan Khaw Sim Bee
Khoo Cheow Teong Court	Halaman Khoo Cheow Teong
Khoo Hye Keat Road	Jalan Khoo Hye Keat
Khoo Sian Ewe Road	Jalan Khoo Sian Ewe
Kim Bian Aik Road	Jalan Kim Bian Aik
Kimberley Street	Lebuh Kimberley
King Edward Place	Pesara King Edward
King Street	Lebuh King
Kinta Lane	Lorong Kinta
Klang Street	Lebuh Klang

Krian Road	Jalan Kerian	Malay Street	Lebuh Melayu
Kuala Kangsar Road	Jalan Kuala Kangsar	Mandalay Road	Jalan Mandalay
Kuantan Road	Jalan Kuantan	Mano Road	Jalan Mano
Kuching Lane	Lorong Kuching	Market Street	Lebuh Pasar
Kuda Road	Jalan Kuda	Maxwell Road	Jalan Maxwell
Kurau Road	Jalan Kurau	Merican Lane	Lorong Merican
		Merican Road	Jalan Merican

L

		Moulmein Road	Jalan Moulmein
		Mount Erskine Road	Jalan Gunung Erskine
Lahat Road	Jalan Lahat	Muda Lane	Lorong Muda
Langkawi Road	Jalan Langkawi	Market Street	Lebuh Pasar
Larut Road	Jalan Larut	Muntri Street	Lebuh Muntri
Leandro's Lane	Lorong Leandro's		
Leith Street	Lebuh Leith		

N

Leith Street Ghaut	Gat Lebuh Leith		
Light Street	Lebuh Light		
Lim Cheng Teik	Medan Lim Cheng Teik	Nagore Road	Jalan Nagor
Square		Nambyar Street	Lebuh Nambyar
		Nanking Road	Jalan Nanking
Lim Eow Thoon Road	Jalan Lim Eow Thoon	New Lane	Lorong Baru
Lim Chin Guan Road	Jalan Lim Chin Guan	Ngah Aboo Lane	Lorong Ngah Aboo
Lim Lean Teng Road	Jalan Lim Lean Teng	Nirvana Road	Jalan Nirvana
Lim Mah Chye Road	Jalan Lim Mah Chye	Noordin Street	Lebuh Noordin
Lines Road	Jalan Lines	Northam Road	Jalan Sultan Ahmad Shah
Logan Road	Jalan Logan	Nunn Road	Jalan Nunn
Loh Boon Siew Road	Jalan Loh Boon Siew		
Lorong Salamat	Lorong Selamat		

O

Lorong Shaik Eusoff	Lorong Shaik Yusoff		
Lorong Susu	Lorong Susu	Ong Chong Keng	Lebuh Ong Chong Keng
Love Lane	Lorong Love	Street	
Lumut Lane	Lorong Lumut		
Lunas Road	Jalan Lunas		

P

		Pahang Road	Jalan Pahang

M

		Panchor Road	Jalan Panchor
		Pangkor Road	Jalan Pangkor
MacAlister Road	Jalan Macalister	Paya Terubong Road	Jalan Paya Terubong
McNair Lane	Lorong Macnair	Parit Buntar Lane	Lorong Parit Buntar
Macallum Street	Lebuh Macallum	Park Road	Jalan Park
Madras Lane	Lorong Madras	Patani Road	Jalan Patani
Magazine Road	Jalan Magazine	Peel Avenue	Lebuhraya Peel
Makloom Road	Jalan Makloom	Peirce Road	Jalan Peirce
Malacca Street	Lebuh Melaka		

Peking Street	Lebuh Peking
Penaga Road	Jalan Penaga
Penang Road	Jalan Penang
Penang Street	Lebuh Pinang
Perak Road	Jalan Perak
Perlis Road	Jalan Perlis
Phee Choon Road	Jalan Phee Choon
Philips Road	Jalan Phillips
Phuah Hin Leong	Jalan Phuah Hin Leong Road
Piggot Road	Jalan Piggot
Pinhorn Road	Jalan Pinhorn
Pitt Street	Jalan Mesjid Kapitan Keling
Popus Lane	Lorong Popus
Presgrave Street	Lebuh Presgrave
Prangin Lane	Lorong Perangin
Prangin Road	Jalan Dr. Lim Chwee Leong
Pulau Tikus Lane	Lorong Pulau Tikus
Pykett Avenue	Lebuhraya Pykett

Q

Quarry Drive	Pesiaran Kuari
Queen Street	Lebuh Queen

R

Race Course Road	Jalan Lumba Kuda
Range Road	Jalan Range
Rangoon Road	Jalan Rangoon
Rawang Road	Jalan Rawang
Reservoir Garden	Taman Kolam Ayer
Residency Road	Jalan Residensi
Rifle Range Road	Jalan Padang Tembak
River Road	Jalan Sungai
Rope Walk	Jalan Pintal Tali
Rose Avenue	Lebuhraya Rose
Ross Road	Jalan Ross

S

Salween Road	Jalan Salween
Sandilands Street	Lebuh Sandilands
Scotland Road	Jalan Scotland
Seck Chuan Lane	Lorong Seck Chuan
School Lane	Lorong Sekolah
Scott Road	Jalan D.S. Ramanathan
Seang Tek Road	Jalan Seang Tek
Seh Tan Court	Halaman Seh Tan
Selama Road	Jalan Selama
Selangor Road	Jalan Selangor
Sepoy Lines Road	Jalan Sepoy Lines
Seremban Lane	Lorong Seremban
Service Road	Jalan Service
Siam Road	Jalan Siam
Singora Lane	Lorong Singgora
Skipton Road	Jalan Skipton
Solok Mas	Solok Mas
Soo Hong Lane	Lorong Soo Hong
Bahari Road	Jalan Sri Bahari
Stadium Circus	Lilitan Stadium
Stewart Lane	Lorong Stewart
Sungei Pinang Pengkalan	Pengkalan Sungai Pinang
Sungai Pinang Road	Jalan Sungai Pinang
Sungai Ujong Road	Jalan Sungai Hujong
Swatow Lane	Lorong Swatow
Swee Lee Grove	Heah Swee Lee Grove

T

Taiping Road	Jalan Taiping
Tamil Street	Lebuh Tamil
Tampin Lane	Lorong Tampin
Tan Iu Ghee Road	Jalan Tan Iu Ghee
Tanjong Bungah Road	Jalan Tanjong Bunga
Tanjong Tokong Road	Jalan Tanjong Tokong
Tavoy Road	Jalan Tavoy
Taylor Road	Jalan Taylor
Tek Soon Street	Lebuh Tek Soon

Thaton Lane	Lorong Thaton
The Esplanade	Padang Esplanade
Thean Teik Road	Jalan Thean Teik
Thomas Road	Jalan Thomas
Thorpe Road	Jalan Thorpe
Timah Road	Jalan Timah
Toh Aka Lane	Lorong Toh Aka
Tongkah Road	Jalan Tongkah
Tramway Road	Jalan Tramway
Trang Road	Jalan Terang
Transfer Road	Jalan Transfer
Trengganu Road	Jalan Trengganu
Trusan Road	Jalan Terusan
Tull Road	Jalan Tull
Tye Kee Yoon Road	Jalan Tye Kee Yoon
Tye Sin Street	Lebuh Tye Sin

Y

Yahudi Road	Jalan Zainal Abidin
Yeoh Guan Seok Road	Jalan Yeoh Guan Seok
York Road	Jalan York
Yeap Chor Ee Road	Jalan Yeap Chor Ee

Z

Jalan Zoo	Zoo Road

U

Udini Road	Jalan Udini
Union Street	Lebuh Union

V

Vale of Tempe Road	Jalan Lembah Permai
Valley Road	Jalan Valley
Van Praagh Road	Jalan Van Praagh
Vermont Road	Jalan Vermont
Victoria Green Road	Jalan Padang Victoria
Victoria Street	Lebuh Victoria

W

Waterfall Road	Jalan Kebun Bunga
Weld Quay	Pengkalan Weld
Wee Hein Tze Road	Jalan Wee Hein Tze
Western Road	Jalan Utama
Westlands Road	Jalan Westlands
Williams Road	Jalan Williams
Wright Road	Jalan Wright
Wu Lien Teh Gardens	Taman Wu Lien Teh

SUBURBAN MAP INDEX

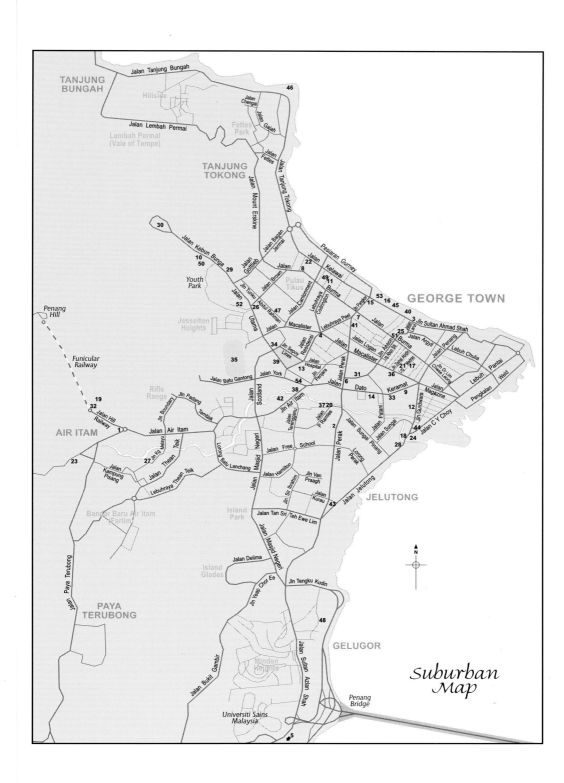

TANJUNG BUNGAH

Jalan Tanjung Bungah

Hillside

Jalan Chengai

Jalan Gajah

46

Jalan Lembah Permai

Lembah Permai (Vale of Tempe)

Fettes Park

Jalan Fettes

TANJUNG TOKONG

Jalan Mount Erskine

Jalan Tanjung Tokong

30

Jalan Kebun Bunga

Pesiaran Gurney

Jalan Bagan Jermal

10
50

29

Youth Park

Jln Tunku Abdul Rahman

Jalan Brown

Jalan Codrington

Jalan

Jalan Kelawai

22

8

Pulau Tikus

49
65
1

Jalan Burma

53
15
16
45

GEORGE TOWN

Jalan Peel

Leburhraya Codrington

7

3
Jln Sultan Ahmad Shah

40

Penang Hill

52
26
47

Jesselton Heights

Jalan Utama

Jalan Macalister

Leburhraya Peel

41

Jalan Logan

Jln Anson

25

Burma

5
Jln Penang

Jalan Argyll

Lebuh Chulia

Funicular Railway

35

34

Jln Sepoy Lines

Jalan Residensi

4

Jalan Hospital

Jln Perak

Jalan Macalister

21
17

Jln Dr Lim Chwe Leong

Lebuh Pantai

39

13

Jalan York

Jln Penjara

6

31

36

Jalan Magazine

Pengkalan

Weld

Lebuh

Jalan Batu Gantong

54

Jalan Dato

14

Keramat

9

33

12

Rifle Range

Jln Padang Tembak

Jalan Scotland

42

Jln Air Itam

37 20

Jalan P Ramlee

Jalan Patani

Jln Gurdwara

Jln C Y Choy

44

19
32
Jalan Hill Railway

38

Jalan Teringganu

Jalan Perak

Jalan Sungai Pinang

18
24

28

AIR ITAM

Jln Kg Melayu

Jalan Thean Teik

Lorong Batu Lanchang

Jalan Majid Negeri

School

Jalan Sungai

27

23

Jalan Kampung Pisang

Jalan Free

Lorong Perak

Lebuhraya Thean Teik

Jalan Hamilton

Jln Van Praagh

Jln Sri Ibrahim

Jalan Kurau

43

Jalan Jelutong

JELUTONG

Island Park

Jalan Tan Sri/Teh Ewe Lim

Jalan Delima

Island Glades

Jalan Majid Negeri

Jln Tengku Kudin

Jalan Paya Terubong

Jln Yeap Chor Ee

48

Jalan Bukit Gambir

PAYA TERUBONG

Minden Heights

Jalan Sultan Azlan Shah

GELUGOR

Penang Bridge

N

Universiti Sains Malaysia

5

suburban Map

CITY MAP INDEX

58 Li Teik Seah Building, Lebuh Carnarvon
59 Logan Memorial, Lebuh Light
60 Logan's Buildings, Lebuh Pantai
61 Loh Leong San's Family Residence, Jalan Burma
62 Loke Thye Kee, Jalan Burma
63 Madrasah Hamid Arabi, Lebuh Ah Quee
64 Mahamariamman Temple, Jalan Mesjid Kapitan Keling
65 Nagore Shrine, Lebuh Chulia
66 Ng See Kah Meow, Lebuh King
67 Noordin Family Tomb, Lebuh Chulia
68 Opium and Spirit Farm Offices, Lebuh Queen
69 Paterson Simons Godowns, Pengkalan Weld
70 Penang Hair-Dressing & Hair-Waving Association, Jalan Prangin
71 Penang Teochew Association, Lebuh Chulia
72 Poe Choo Seah, Lebuh King
73 Prangin Road Market, Gat Lebuh Prangin
74 Protestant Cemetery, Jalan Sultan Ahmad Shah
75 Runnymede, Jalan Sultan Ahmad Shah
76 San Wooi Wooi Koon, Lebuh Bishop
77 Seh Ong Kongsi, Jalan Penang
78 Seh Teoh Kongsi, Lebuh Carnarvon
79 Seri Rambai, Lebuh Light
80 Sheikh Omar's Residence, Lebuh Acheh
81 Sheikh Zachariah Basheer & Sons, Lorong Lumut
82 Shih Chung School, Jalan Sultan Ahmad Shah
83 Soo Beng Dispensary, Jalan Dr. Lim Chwee Leong
84 Standard Chartered Bank, Lebuh Pantai
85 State Assembly Buildings, Lebuh Light
86 Penang State Museum, Lebuh Farquhar
87 St. George's Church, Lebuh Farquhar
88 St. Xavier's Church, Jalan Penang
89 Sun Tak Association, Lorong Love
90 Supreme Court Building, Lebuh Farquhar
91 Syed Alatas Mansion, Lebuh Armenian
92 Toi San Nin Yong Hui Kwon & Wu Ti Meow, Lebuh King
93 Tseng Lung Fui Kon, Lebuh King
94 Tua Pek Kong Temple, Lebuh King
95 United Association of Cantonese Districts, Lebuh Chulia
96 United Muslim Association, Jalan Transfer
97 Victoria Memorial Clock Tower, Pesara King Edward
98 Wing Look Restaurant, Jalan Penang
99 Wisma Kastam, Gat Lebuh China
100 Yap Kongsi, Lebuh Armenian
101 Yen Keng Hotel, Lebuh Chulia
102 Yeoh Kongsi, Gat Lebuh Chulia
103 Yin Oi Tong, Lebuh Penang

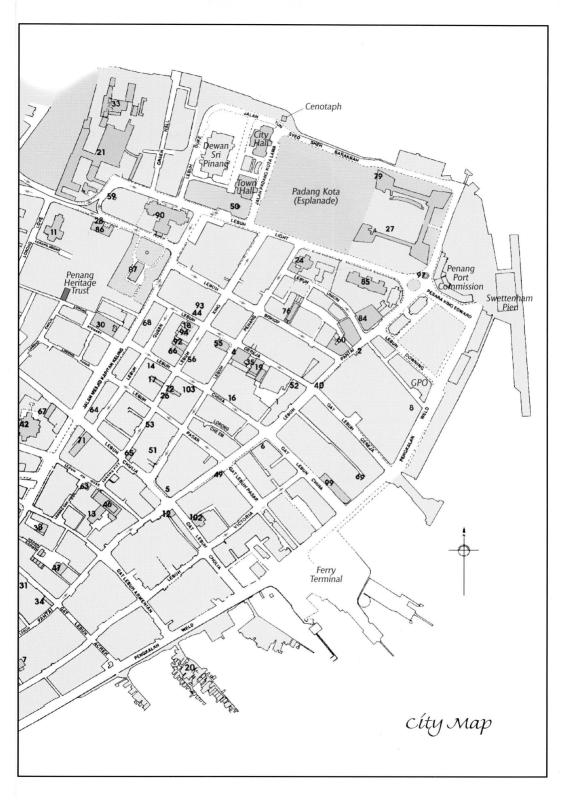

City Map

ABOUT THE AUTHOR

Khoo Su Nin @ Khoo Salma Nasution was born, bred and schooled in Penang. She is a graduate of Duke University, former Editor of Pulau Pinang Magazine, and currently principal of the publication design firm Janus Print & Resources. As the great-great granddaughter of Khoo Soo Hong, a founding senator of the Leong San Tong Khoo Kongsi, she has her roots in the Acheen Street-Armenian Street historic-cultural enclave. She works from the 1870s shophouse at 120 Armenian Street which once served as Dr. Sun Yat Sen's Penang Base.

She is currently working as a free-lance writer and community heritage consultant:
- Honorary Secretary of Penang Heritage Trust since 1989
- Co-founder of the Asia & West Pacific Network for Urban Conservation (AWPNUC) in 1991 and currently the editor
- Project Manager, Syed Alatas Mansion restoration (1993-4)
- Coordinator, Sustainable Penang Initiative (1997-1999), participatory approach to sustainable development planning.

Together with husband Abdur-Razzaq Lubis:
- Parents of two lovely children
- Researchers, The Toyota Foundation funded project on history of Mandailing migration (1997-present)
- Produced heritage maps on Taiping (1998), Ipoh (1999)
- Site managers for a UNESCO-LEAP funded project called "Community Participation in Waqf Revitalization", 1999.